James Westfall T

The Development

of the

French Monarchy

under Louis VI. Le Gros

1108-1137

Elibron Classics
www.elibron.com

THE DEVELOPMENT

OF THE

FRENCH MONARCHY

UNDER LOUIS VI. LE GROS

1108–1137

A DISSERTATION PRESENTED TO THE FACULTY OF ARTS
LITERATURE, AND SCIENCE OF THE UNIVERSITY
OF CHICAGO, IN CANDIDACY FOR THE
DEGREE OF DOCTOR OF
PHILOSOPHY

BY

JAMES WESTFALL THOMPSON, A.B.

CHICAGO
The University of Chicago Press
1895

CONTENTS.

BIBLIOGRAPHY.

The following list is as exhaustive a bibliography as could be compiled. In the nature of things it could be amplified by researches in the Bibliothèque Nationale. No one who has not learned them from his own experience, can realize the difficulties under which an American student labors, in making a thorough study of European — and especially mediæval history, so far from the sphere of action. Hitherto, in Graduate Schools, the emphasis has been almost wholly laid upon American history and institutions.

Almost all the chronicles cited may be found in the *Recueil des Historiens des Gaules et de la France*, Paris, 1738–1876, 23 vols. Edited by Bouquet, Brial, Pardessus, Delisle, and others. Tomes XII. to XV. contain the sources of the period under consideration. Reference to these volumes have been cited simply "H. F." In chronicles or letters of special importance, fuller indication is made. The most important

NARRATIVE SOURCES.

Sugerius, *Vita Ludovici VI. Grossi sive Crassi regis, Philippi I. filii.* Edition of Molinier. *Collection de Textes de la Société de l'École des Chartes.* Paris, 1887. This is uniformly cited unless that of the *Société de l'Histoire de France* is mentioned. The latter is:

SUGERIUS, *Vita Ludovici VI. Grossi, etc.*

— Liber de Rebus sua administratione gestis.

WILLELMUS, *Vita Sugerii, abbatis S. Dionysii.* Edition of Lecoy de la Marche. Paris, 1867.

ORDERICUS VITALIS, *Historica Ecclesiastica. Société de l'Histoire de France.* Edition of Leprevost, 5 vols. Paris, 1838–55.

GALBERTUS BRUGENSIS, *Passio Karoli comitis Flandriae. Collection de Textes de la Société de l'École des Chartes,* Edition of Pirenne. Paris 1891.

Chronicon Morigniacensis Monasterii, ord. S. Benedicti, H. F., XII.

HENRICI HUNTENDUNSIS, *Historia Anglorum,* Edition of Arnold, Rolls Series. London, 1879.

WILLELMI MALMSBIRIENSIS, *De Gestis Regum Anglorum,* Edition of Stubbs, Rolls Series, 2 vols., *Ibid.* London, 1887.

vii

DOCUMENTARY SOURCES.

Epistolae Ludovici VI., H. F., XV.
— *Sugerii*   "   "
— *St. Bernardi*   "   "
— *Ivonis Carnotensis,*   "   *XII.*

LUCHAIRE, *Louis VI. (le Gros)*; *Annales de sa Vie et de son Règne (1081-1137), avec une Introduction historique.* Paris, 1890.

Ordonnances des Rois de France de la IIIe race jusqu'en 1514. 22 vols., Paris, 1723-1849. Tomes I, VII, XI, XII.

TARDIF, *Monuments historiques,* 2 vols., Paris, 1866.

TEULET, *Layettes du Trésor des Chartes,* 3 vols., Paris, 1863, Vol. I.

VIOLLET, *Une Grande Chronique latine de Saint Denis. Observations pour servir à l'histoire critique des Oeuvres de Suger,* in *Bibliothèque de l'École des Chartes,* XXXIV, 1873.

ROBERT, *Histoire et bullaire du pape Calixte II.* (1119-1124). *Essai de Restitution.* 2 vols., Paris, 1891.

LANGLOIS, *Textes Relatifs à l'Histoire du Parlement depuis les Origines jusqu'en 1314. Collection de Textes de la Société de l'École des Chartes* Paris, 1888.

MABILLON, *De Re Diplomatica.* Second Edition. Paris, 1709.

BRUSSEL, *Nouvel Examen de l'Usage général des fiefs en France.* 2 vols., Paris, 1727.

Collection de documents inédits sur l'Histoire de France.

GUERARD, *Cartulaire de l'Église Notre-Dame de Paris.* 4 vols. Paris, 1850.
— *Cartulaire de St. Denis,* 6 vols. Paris, 1839-1852.
— *Cartulaire de l'abbaye de Saint Père à Chartres.* 2 vols. Paris, 1840.

DU CANGE, *Glossarium,* New Edition, 10 vols. Paris, 1883.

AUTHORITIES.

LUCHAIRE, *Histoire des Institutions Monarchiques de la France sous les premiers Capétiens,* (987-1180). 2 vols. Second Edition. Paris, 1891. Contains Appendix of original documents.
— *Manuel des Institutions Françaises.* Paris, 1892.
— *Les Communes Françaises a l'Époque des Capétiens directs.* Paris, 1890.
— *La Cour du Roi et ses fonctions judiciaires sous le Règne de Louis VI.* (1108-1137), in *Annales de la Faculté des Lettres de Bourdeaux,* 1880.
— *Remarques sur la Succession des Grands Officiers de la Couronne,* (1108-1180). In *Annales de la Faculté des Lettres de Bourdeaux,* 1881.

VIOLLET, *Histoire du Droit Français.* Paris, 1886.

FLACH, *Les Origines de l'ancienne France.* 2 vols. Paris, 1886.

COMBES, *L'Abbé Suger: Histoire de son Ministère et de sa Régence.* Paris, 1853.

HUGUENIN, *Étude sur l'abbé Suger.* Paris, 1855.

ROBERT, *Histoire du Pape Calixte II.* Paris, 1891.

VUITRY, *Études sur le Régime financier de la France avant la Revolution de 1789.* 3 vols. Paris, 1878-1883. Vol. I.

PARDESSUS, *Essai Historique sur l'Organisation judiciaire et l'Administration de la justice.* Paris, 1851.

HENRION, *De l'Autorité judiciaire en France.* Paris, 1827.

DULAURE, *Histoire de Paris.* Paris, 1829. (Fourth Edition).

BRÉQUIGNY, *Recherches sur les Communes et les Bourgeoisies.* Preface to *Recueil des Historiens des Gaules et de la France,* tomes XI, XII.

GROSS, *Gild Merchant.* 2 vols. Oxford, 1890.

DANIEL, *Histoire de la Milice française et des Changements qui s'y sont faits depuis l'établissement de la Monarchie française dans les Gaules jusqu'à la fin du Règne de Louis le Grand.* 2 vols. Amsterdam, 1724.

GAILLARD, *Histoire de la Rivalité de la France et de l'Angleterre.* 6 vols. Paris, 1818. Vol. I.

LAMPRECHT, *Étude sur l'État économique de la France pendant la première partie du Moyen-Age.* Translated by A. Marignan. Paris, 1889.

BOUTARIC, *Institutions Militaires de la France.* Paris, 1863.

GLASSON, *Histoire Du Droit des Institutions de la France.* To be complete in ten volumes. Paris, 1884, ff. Vols. IV-V.

IMBART DE LA TOUR, *Les Élections épiscopales dans l'Église de France du IXe au XIIIe Siècles.* Paris, 1891.

BARON DE NERVO, *Les Finances françaises sous l'ancienne Monarchie, la République, la Consulat et l'Empire.* 3. vols. Paris, 1863. Vol. I.

EMILE LAIR, *Des Hautes Cours Politiques en France et à l'Étranger.* Paris, 1889.

GUIZOT, *History of Civilization in France.* New York. Hazlitt's Translation. Many editions.

RAMBAUD, *Histoire de la Civilisation française.* 2 vols. Fifth Edition. Paris, 1893.

GIESEBRECHT, *Geschichte der deutschen Kaiserzeit.* 5 vols. Vol. III., Fifth Edition. Leipzig, 1890.

PFISTER, *Études sur le Régne de Robert le Pieux,* Paris 1885.

PETIT, *Histoire des Ducs de Bourgogne de la Race capétienne.* 5 vols. Dijon, 1885. Vol. I.

CHEVALIER, *Repertoire des sources historiques du Moyen-Age*—Bio-bibliographie.

DARESTE, *Histoire de l'Administration et des progrès du pouvoir royal en France.* 2 vols. Paris, 1848.

C. P. MARIE-HAAS, *L'Administration de la France.* Four volumes in two. Paris, 1861. Vol. I.

AUBERT, *Le Parlement de Paris de Philippe le Bel à Charles VII.* (1314–1422). Paris, 1886.

FREEMAN, *History of the Norman Conquest of England.* 5 vols. Third Edition. Oxford, 1876–1877. Vol. V.

— *The Reign of William Rufus.* 2. vols. Oxford, 1882.

STUBBS, *Constitutional History of England.* 3 vols. Fifth Edition. Oxford, 1891. Vol. I.

PALGRAVE, *History of England and Normandy.* 4 vols. Vol. IV. London, 1864.

RANKE, *Franzosische Geschichte. Werke,* VIII.

NORGATE, *England under the Angevin Kings.* 2 vols. London, 1887.

WALKER, *On the Increase of Royal Power in France under Philip Augustus.* Leipzig. 1888.

THIERRY, *Histoire du Tiers-État.* Paris, 1853.

— *Lettres sur l'Histoire de France.* Seventh Edition. Paris, 1859.

RAYNOUARD, *Histoire du Droit Municipal en France.* Paris, 1829. 2 vols.

CLAMAGERAN, *Histoire de l'Impôt en France.* 2 vols. Paris, 1867.

PIGEONNEAU, *Histoire du Commerce de la France.* 2 vols. Paris, 1889.

LEVASSEUR, *Histoire des Classes Ouvrières en France.* 4 vols. Paris, 1859.

BRENTANO, *Introduction to Montchretien, Traité de l'Œconomie politique.* Paris, 1889.

BRENTANO, *On the History and Development of Gilds.* London, 1870.

SCHAEFFNER, *Geschichte der Rechtsverfassung Frankreichs.* 4 vols. Frankfort, 1845-9. Vol. 2.

LEA, *History of Sacerdotal Celibacy.* Philadelphia, 1886.

LANGLOIS, *Le Règne de Phillippe le Hardi.* Paris, 1887.

SECRETAN, *Essai sur la Féodalité.* Lausanne, 1858.

LAURENT, *La Féodalité et l'Église.* Second Edition. Paris, 1865.

Bibliothèque des Hautes Études ·

GIRY, *Histoire de la Ville de Saint Omer.* Paris, 1877.

— *Établissements de Rouen.* 2 vols. Paris, 1885.

LE FRANC, *Histoire de la Ville de Noyen.* Paris 1887.

WAUTERS, *Les Libertés Communales. Essai sur leur origines et leurs premiers développements en Belgique, dans le Nord de la France et sur les bords du Rhin.* 2 vols. Bruxelles, 1872.

TAILLAR, *Notice sur l'origine de la formation des villages du Nord de la France.* Douai, 1862.

HIRSCH, *Studien zur Geschichte Konig Ludwigs VII. von Frankreich* (1119–1160). Leipzig, 1892.

LALANNE, *Dictionnaire historique.* Second Edition. Paris, 1887.

CHERUEL, *Dictionnaire historique des Institutions de la France.* 2 vols. Paris, 1880.

HENAULT, *Abrégé Chronologique de l'Histoire de France.* 2 vols. Paris, 1823.

LONGNON, *Atlas historique de la France.* Troisième Livraison. Paris, 1889.

PHILLIPS, *Der Ursprung des Regalienrechts in Frankreich.* Halle, 1870.

THIEL, *Die politische Thatigkeit des Abtes Bernhard von Clairvaux.*

HORES, *Das Bistum Cambrai, seine polit. und kirchl. Beziehungen zu Deutschland, Frankreich und Flandern, und Entwicklung der Commune von Cambrai* (1092–1191). Leipzig, 1882.

SPECIAL ARTICLES, OR ESSAYS.

REVUE DE DEUX MONDES, Oct., 1873, p. 581. *Origines de l'Administration royale en France.*

REVUE HISTORIQUE, XXXVII. (1888). Luchaire. *Louis le Gros et son Palatins.*

REVUE HISTORIQUE, XLII. (1890). Langlois: *Les Origines du Parlement de Paris.*

REVUE HISTORIQUE, XLIV. (1890). Piou: *De la Nature du Service militaire par les Roturiers aux XIe et XIIe siècles.*

REVUE HISTORIQUE, XLIX. (1892). Leroux: *La Royauté française et le Saint Empire Romain.*

REVUE DES QUESTIONS HISTORIQUES, XLIX. Vacandard: *St. Bernard et la Royauté française.*

NOUVELLE REVUE HISTORIQUE DE DROIT FRANÇAIS ET ÉTRANGÉR, VIII. (1884) pp. 139, 267, 441. Prou: *Les Coutumes de Lorris et leur propagation aux XIIe et XIIIe siècles.*

MÉMOIRES DE L'ACADÉMIE DES INSCRIPTIONS·

XXVII. 184 (1754). Lebeuf: *Éclaircissements sur la chronologie des règnes de Louis le Gros et de Louis le Jeune.*

XXIX. 268 (1760). Bonamy: *Remarques sur le titre de Très-Chrétien donné aux rois de France, et sur le temps où cet usage a commencé.*

XXIX. 273 (1760). Bonamy: *Recueil d'autorités qui servent à prouver que longtemps avant le règne de Louis XI. nos rois ont été décorés du titre de Très-Chrétien.*

XLIII. 345 (1777). Gaillard: *Des Causes de la haine personelle qu'on a cru remarqué entre Louis VI. et Henri I., roi d'Angleterre.*

XLIII. 421 (1778). Bréquigny: *Observations sur le testament de Guillaume X., duc d'Aquitaine et comte de Poitou, mort en 1137.*

IV. 489 (1805). Brial: *Recherches historiques et diplomatiques sur la véritable époque de l'association de Louis le Gros au trône avec le titre de Roi désigné.*

VII. 129 (1806). Brial: *Éclaircissement d'un passage de l'abbé Suger relatif à l'histoire du Berry.*

IX. (1886). Luchaire: *Sur deux monogrammes de Louis le Gros.*

SÉANCES ET TRAVAUX DE L'ACADÉMIE DES SCIENCES MORALES ET POLITIQUES:

XVI. 161 (1888). Luchaire: *Les Milices communales et la Royauté capétienne.*

GENERAL HISTORIES.

MARTIN, *Histoire de France.* 17 vols. Paris, 1840.

SISMONDI, *Histoire des Français.* 31 vols. Paris, 1821–1844.

MICHELET, *Histoire de France.* 17 vols. Paris, 1871–1874.

MABLY, *Collection complète des Oeuvres de l'abbé Mably.* 15 vols. Paris, 1794–1795. Vol. 2.

VELLY, VILLARET, GARNIER, etc., *Histoire de France.* 26 vols. Paris, 1808–1812.

KITCHEN, *History of France.* Third Edition. Oxford, 1892. 3 vols. Vol. I.

Popular but wholly uncritical works, or articles, are:

DeCarne, *Fondateurs de l'Unité Française.* 2 vols. 1856. "*Suger.*"

Baudrillart, *Histoire du Luxe.* 4 vols. Paris, 1881. Vol. III., ch. v., "*Suger et son rôle dans le luxe.*"

Clement, in *Le Moniteur Universel,* 1853, pp. 1391, 1395, 1427. December 16, 17, 25, 1853. "*Portraits Historiques—Suger.*"

Other writings which will be at once recognized are occasionally cited, but the body of the dissertation has been built upon the above.

INTRODUCTION.

LOUIS VI. AND THE FRENCH MONARCHY.

" M. Thierry remarks very truly that every people has two histories — the one interior, national and domestic, the other exterior. The former he goes on to describe as the history of its laws and institutions, and its political changes — in one word, of its action upon itself; the latter he refers to the action of the people upon others, and the part it may claim in influencing the common destinies of the world. Of these two histories the first cannot, of course, be fully written till the people has reached the term of its political individuality, neither can the second be written till the farthest effect of its influence can be traced and estimated."[1]

These words are profound political philosophy. The first category eminently characterizes the history of mediæval France, at least until the reign of Philip Augustus, when France was nearing the term of her political individuality and was beginning to appear upon the wide arena of European politics. In order properly to understand the growth of a state we must consider it in its origin and termination. Between these limits all is formative, institutional. The Middle Ages were essentially an institutional period, when forms and customs were in the making. They were the gigantic crucible into which all the greatness and grandeur of the ancient civilized world was plunged; they were the crucible out of which the states and nations and institutions of modern Europe emerged. Among these institutions there was one which was all-prevalent: feudalism, in ever-varying form, was *the* institution of the Middle Ages.[2]

[1] Merivale. *History of the Romans under the Empire.* Fourth edition, 1863. Vol. I. Introd., p. 8, citing Amedée Thierry.

[2] Yet feudalism does not present the phenomena of social decay, but of social progress. It was an attempt to regulate the disorder due to the weak-

1

Feudalism is the accompaniment of a declining civilization. When a great state is passing into decadence, class interests usurp the higher, public interests and authority. The Frank monarchy was organized under feudal forms because the political features of Teutonic life had become more or less assimilated with those of the decaying Roman *imperium.* When the Romano-Frank monarchy also declined, the feudal régime was intensified in degree. And yet, during the entire tenth century, when its power was least, the Carlovingian dynasty struggled to maintain the traditional character of the monarchy, and was, as a consequence, in antagonism with the excessive feudal tendency. More than this—all the kings of this century, whether they appertained to the Carlovingian house or to the family of Robert the Strong, sought with varying energy and unequal success to maintain the prerogatives of monarchial authority against the encroachments of feudalism. This was a steadfast purpose in the mind of the representatives of the rival houses, as well those who were kings as those who sought to be kings. The difference lay in this: the Carlovingian monarchy reposed on past traditions, past persons, past powers. The glamor of the great days of the great Charles tinged it with an alienated majesty and made it seem, to the infatuated minds of Louis IV. and Lothar, what it was not. This accounts for Louis' rash attempt to conquer Normandy, and Lothar's equally rash effort to recover Lotharingia. The age was not as great as their ideas. On the other hand, the house of Robert was self-reliant. It had no force not of itself on which to rely; it had no taint of outworn sovereignty. Moreover, the personal force of Robert and Odo and the two Hughs was superior to the personal force of their royal rivals, although that was not as despicable as is customarily believed.[1]

The later Carlovingians were not weak ; they were not deficient in activity and energy. The legend that they were morally weak is due partly to the natural analogy between the last days of the Merovingians and the Carlovingians, and also to a failure to

ness of government. For some wise words on this head, see Stubbs, *Bened. Peterburg.* (Rolls Series), II. Introd. xxxv.

[1] Luchaire, *Inst. Mon.,* I., 27.

observe with due regard that time and circumstance wonderfully modify the face of events. This is one reason. Partly also because it is the irony of history that men who fight a losing cause almost never — Hannibal is a sovereign exception — however great be their efforts, win admiration. Louis d'Outremer and Lothar were men of approved courage, perseverance and a moral superiority above their immediate predecessors. The trouble was that they tried to do too much. They used their resources with a vigor and lavishness which, if they had moved with the current would have made them princes great indeed. But the alienated majesty of the empire, the vast continuity of force which had never been balked from Pepin d'Heristal and Charles Martel downwards till the day of Louis Debonnaire, made these later kings of the same house ill brook a substitution of suzerainty for sovereignty.

The responsibility of this new situation lies more at the feet of the earlier successors of Charles the Great. If Louis Debonnaire dissolved the sheaf of his authority and suffered the grain to be taken, what could his successors do with the straw? It was a difficult thing to build up power upon a bundle of negatives, and this state of things was aggravated by the coming of the Northmen. The later Carlovingians were obliged to accept the results of the triple revolution which tended to suppress the central power, *in fact*, though they saved their dignity by not doing so *in law*, namely: (1) The transformation of the benefice in fief. (2) The usurpation and hereditary transmission of public functions. (3) The hierarchichal constitution of feudalism, which tended to make the king more a suzerain than a sovereign.[1]

The cardinal errors of the Carlovingians were twofold:

1. A failure to direct the revolution, working itself out in process of time, which they might have done. They tried to stem the current and hence were swept where the current listed.

2. A failure to confine themselves to the limits assigned by treaty of Verdun. The bauble of empire was too attractive to Charles the Bald. Lothar wasted his strength in a vain effort to recover Lotharingia. He asserted the sterile pretensions of a

[1] Luchaire, *Inst. Mon.*, I., 28.

bygone royalty, instead of seeking to keep that that he had a compact whole. It was his interest to keep the royal domain, as much as possible a solid political entity, with a vast circumscription of feudal groups. A homogeneous territorial basis for royalty would have been the surest and most material aid for a gradual and progressive increase of royal power. But a solid territorial basis is exactly what the Carlovingians lacked, and exactly what their successors had. The Carlovingians were, in 987, neither proprietors nor vassals. Louis V. was lord of Laon, but only a tenant at will,[1] while Hugh Capet was proprietor of a goodly portion of Gaul. This central position of his domain was a most substantial fact in his favor. The territorial disproportion between the positions of the two was what shifted the balance of power, at Senlis, on that day in July 987, for Hugh Capet had lands, money and men.[2]

The election of Hugh Capet was not a political and social revolution, assuring the triumph of the feudal polity, much less a national movement. It was hardly more than a change of dynasty, inspired and realized by the church in order to establish in the hands of a powerful feudal family the Romano-Frank ecclesiastical monarchy of the west Carlovingians. The revolution of 987 made the Frank monarchy (for it was not yet *French*) a vivid reality and not a phantom. As that was, it was, a monarchy by divine right, absolute in principle and *theoretically* uniting the powers and prerogatives of sovereignty. It cannot be said that the accession of the house of Capet to the throne marks the beginning of a new monarchy in harmony with the new social state. The view that the revolution of 987 was meant to

[1] Richer, II., 51.

[2] "Two of the great rivers of Gaul, the Seine and the Loire, flowed through the royal domains, but the king was wholly cut off from the sea. . . . . Thus surrounded by their own vassals the early kings of the house of Paris had far less dealings with powers beyond their own kingdom than their Carlovingian predecessors. They were thus able to make themselves the great power of Gaul before they stood forth in a wide field as one of the powers of Europe." Freeman, *Hist. Geog.*, I., 3 ff.

On the extent of Hugh Capet's lands and the character of the ducal title see Pfister, *Le Règne de Robert le Pieux*, livre II., chap. iii.

harmonize, and so did the unity of the realm with the partition of sovereignty, that it was the simultaneous and equal expression of each, is plausible, but not true. Hugh Capet and his successors, in word and deed, sought to act as kings, and did so, save in so far as they were limited by the intervention of the great barons. But they were wise enough not to try to do more than they were able. They knew their powers and were content to exercise them within the limits of efficiency.

The accident of birth deprived the early Capetians of that "divinity which doth hedge a king"—that impalpable force which time alone can bring—but this moral deficiency was largely compensated for by the material power at their command. The barons elected Odo and Rudolph and finally Hugh, because each united material possession and moral force. When Hugh was elected, he became heir to all the imprescriptible rights and indefinable privileges which attended his predecessor.

"The king had a whole arsenal of rights: Old rights of Carlovingian royalty, preserving the remembrance of imperial power, which the study of the Roman law was to resuscitate, transforming these apparitions into formidable realities; old rights conferred by coronation which were impossible to define and hence incontestable; and rights of suzerainty, newer and more real, which were definitely determined and codified, as feudalism developed, and which joined to the other rights mentioned above, made the king proprietor of France. These are the elements that Capetian royalty contributed to the play of fortuitous circumstances. Everything turned to his profit: the miseries of the church, which, in the midst of a violent society claimed the royal protection, from one end of the kingdom to the other, and also the efforts of the middle classes to be admitted with defined rights into feudal society. . . . . His (the king's) authority was thus exercised outside the limits of his own particular domain, throughout the whole kingdom." [1]

The monarchy founded by Hugh Capet partook of a double character. He was the greatest feudal lord on the soil of Gaul

[1] Lavisse, *General View of Political History of Europe.* (English Translation, New York, 1891, p. 61.)

before he inherited the domain of the ancient kings, their rights, and the prestige attached to the idea of royalty. Thus when he became king he was stronger than his immediate predecessors. He was the heir of past power and place, with also, be it said, the deficiencies attending that estate in later years; but he was also the holder of inchoate and potential rights, destined to be worked out in the process of feudalization and the progress of kingship.

The edifice of Capetian royal authority of which Robert the Strong laid the foundation, and to which Hugh Capet annexed the capstone, was made of various elements.

1. It consisted of the mass of proprietary rights, which were bound up in the sheaf of his feudal superiority, whether as immediate or indirect lord.

2. It comprised all the historic rights and privileges of the former Carlovingian kings — political and ecclesiastical, theoretical and actual.

3. Hugh Capet's title of *dux Francorum*, conferred new rights of a particular character, which in 987 were blended with his royal authority.

Although predominantly feudal, the French monarchy had a double character. Its theories and its practices were to a considerable degree royal. In addition to those old rights of Carlovingian royalty; in addition to other ancient rights conferred by coronation and the newer and more real rights of suzerainty, there were certain specific rights which the king had from the beginning: (1) The nominal if not efficient right of regulating public benefices. (2) The ascription of public authority.[1] (3) The *regale*, too, was less a feudal than a royal prerogative.

The king's ecclesiastical sovereignty conveyed in the term *regale* was never so divided as his political authority. Some remnants of supremacy were left in localities not forming a portion of the royal domain. This state of things was a result of the historical combination of circumstances. The church was

---

[1] "It was accepted, theoretically as a fundamental principle, that no crown vassal could lawfully carry on war, otherwise than immediately under his sovereign or by royal command" (Palgrave, *History of England and Normandy*, III., 52).

the depository of the Roman tradition of unity and centralization, taken up and continued by the Merovingians and Austra-
sians, which in the form of a semi-ecclesiastical imperial authority
culminated in Charles the Great. In the break-up of the Empire,
this regalian principle escaped the shipwreck of the Carlovingian
dynasty owing to the integrity of the ecclesiastical constitution
which preserved the lines of bishoprics and metropolitanates.
The Church, in spite of feudal infiltration, was less impaired
than any other institution and received a large accession of
power in the tenth century when the revolution of 987 was
carried to a successful issue by the great churchmen of Gaul.
Thereby it was predetermined that the church and the king
should coöperate in the development of the French monarchy.

This relation existing between the throne and the Gallican
Church was never positively broken. The bond was often
severely strained but it was never ruptured. Meanwhile, the
kings, being defenders of the church in their realm against the
turbulence and avarice of the baronage, insisted that royal jurisdiction applied alike to secular and ecclesiastical affairs. In the
eleventh century, however, the royal power reached its lowest
point and feudal usurpations grew more common, so that, owing
to continued vexations, the kings came to recognize the right of
the bishops with their chapters, the chapters with the abbeys, the
archdeacons with the prevots or canons of the churches. But
the rights of each party were so illy defined in the Middle Ages,
their efficacy depended so much upon personal energy and will,
that the crown never lost absolutely, nor did the clergy or great
lay lords ever gain wholly, the disputed prerogative.[1]

One naturally recurs to Germany in considering this question
of the *regale*. It was not due to the good character of the
Gallican bishops, when compared with their German brethren,
that Gaul was spared the conflict that rent the empire asunder.
In France the pope already had a measure of authority and was
therewith content; while in Germany he was driven to antagonism because the imperiousness of emperors like Henry III. abso-

[1] *Revue Hist.*, XLII. (1890). Langlois, *Les Origines du Parlement de Paris*, 87.

lutely barred him out. Another reason will also explain the difference between Gaul and Germany in this quarrel. In Germany, *all* the bishoprics were at the disposal of the emperor. In Gaul, this right was distributed among the feudal lords. Thus the power of the king over the church was less redoubtable, and the pope having less to fear, had less cause to contest the royal prerogative. This comparative immunity afforded the French kings an opportunity to develop their ecclesiastical authority to such a point that when the popes at last did try to assert Gregorian pretensions, his own power was shivered for his pains.

If the king's position, however, differed in *kind* and not in degree merely from that of the baronage, the king was yet, at the same time, by his quality as suzerain, by his official and private relations with the aristocracy, profoundly involved in the mesh of the feudal régime. His suzerainty even was for a long time more theoretical than real. The Capetian monarchy so far submitted to the seigneurial régime as to become far more feudal than royal. Yet the theory of royal authority remained with the monarchy. In the tenth and eleventh centuries feudal force was stronger than royal theory. But the day came with Louis VI., and even Louis VII., weak as he was, and Philip Augustus, when the acts of the crown began to modify the feudal régime. Then the theories were active sources of power, for they gave the monarchy a basis of legality upon which to operate.[1]

The feudal régime in Gaul attained its ultimate form in the eleventh century. But it is not to be forgotten that epochs and eras shade into one another. There are few cataclysms in historical development like the swift volcanic formations of the geologic world. History works itself out in a series of degradations and a corresponding series of ascensions; on the stepping-stones of its dead self the world rises to higher things. We are

---

[1] There is no philosophical study, in English, of these features of the Capetian monarchy. The reader is referred to Luchaire, *Inst. Mon.*, I., livre I. Flach, *Les Origines de l'ancienne France*, Vol. I., which contains a good deal of value, but the observations are scattered. The best account is Pfister, *Le Règne de Robert le Pieux*, livre II.

apt to believe that the era of the Carlovingian decline was chaotic ; and yet there are a few rare lights traversing the gloom of that gigantic *mêlée* of peoples, and races, and languages, and manners, and faiths, and institutions. The tangled star-dust of a dissolving world rounds into new forms, and finally a new world emerges, occupying the centuries lying between the ninth and the fifteenth centuries, *i. e.*, the six centuries of feudal Europe.

We are apt to think of feudalism as a hard and fast mould into which Europe was poured and held, as in a strait-jacket. Yet the real truth is that the characteristic of the age is its instability. The relations of man and man in the same region differ. This particularism everywhere dominant makes every case an exception. The relation of man and man has not the force of a sanctioned principle. Local customs are not written ; they are essentially mobile until they are hardened into form by the will of some petty despot. And yet out of this reign of individual absolutism, circumscribed perhaps by the *banlieue* merely, was to come forth an absolutism the most absolute, and circumscribed only by the limits of France. The history of the transition from the scattered sovereignty of Hugh Capet to the self-centred absolutism of Louis XIV. is the history of the progress of a policy never exceeded for consistency of execution, craft in application and patience in development.

Because the French monarchy did become so absolute we are apt to believe it became so by sheer force. The word "absolute" is misleading — we think of tyrants like Ivan the Terrible of Russia, and the praetorian guard of the Cæsars. But the French absolutism was not built up, like the Roman *imperium*, by the power of the sword.[1] We are apt to think that the king grew strong because, as chance availed, he usurped the right to do such and such a thing. But the French monarchy was a *reign of law* throughout. The reign of Louis IX. was splendid in its achievements, yet he never took one ounce of new power or an ascription of authority, or one rood of land, without legal sanction.

[1] The Ordonnance of Orleans (1439) of Charles VII. is really almost the conclusion of absolutism.

Even the unscrupulous kings like Philip Augustus and Philip the Fair covered their conduct with the guise of law. By fictions and technicalities they contrived to give the monarchy a sanction for its acts. This strictly legal character of the development of the French monarchy is a point which has received far too little attention. It is essential to keep this legal phase in mind, for only by so doing can its evolution be truly understood.

In the feudal principle, however, lay alike the weakness and the strength of the early Capetian monarchy. Jealousy of the over-lord on the part of a half hundred petty princes forced the crown to move guardedly. But in the slowness of the growth of the crown was the assurance of its permanence. Absorption of powers on the part of royalty was so gradual that the barons failed to see, until too late, the import of a movement, which, while evolutionary in process, was revolutionary in effect.

The increase of royal power in France involved three processes : (1) The recognition of the hereditary principle in succession. (2) The transfer of all sovereign functions to the crown. (3) The incorporation of fiefs.

In the tenth century the principle of succession by inheritance had hardly enough force to legitimize it in the eyes of men of the time. A curious phenomenon comes to light. Hugh Capet became king by elective right, the address of Archbishop Adalberon setting forth the legitimacy of elective monarchy, and repudiating the doctrine of hereditary right to the throne.[1] And yet we see that at once the progress of events begins gradually to push aside the theory. The kings of the Capetian house during more than three centuries had male offspring ; and, as always happens, out of the fact developed a law—that of hereditary succession. But the uncertainty of the right explains why the first six kings compromised, so to speak, with the elective principle, and took the precaution of always securing the coronation of their successors in their lifetime (coöptation),[2] until by the time

[1] Richer IV., c. 11.

[2] Luchaire, *Inst. Mon.*, I., 59, points out that association upon the throne was also practiced by the later Carlovingians, at least by Lothar in 979.

Nevertheless, the idea of hereditary right excited a certain degree of

of Philip Augustus the triumph of the hereditary principle in succession over the principle of election was assured beyond peradventure.

The second element—the transfer of royal functions to the crown—took place simultaneously with the third—that of the incorporation of fiefs. As royal feudalism grew, the kings seized the chance of annexing lands immediately adjoining the duchy of France. As the means of exercising sovereignty increased, the territorial extent of sovereignty increased also.[1]

The history of feudal France comprises three periods:

1. The period of dominant feudalism (887–1108)—that of the later Carlovingians and early Capetians.

2. The period of the triumph of the hereditary principle in succession to the throne, and that in which feudalism is seriously impaired by the crown (1108–1314)—from the reign of Louis le Gros to the death of Philip the Fair.

3. The triumph of the absolute monarchy and the evolution of the modern state (1314–1483)—from the death of Philip the Fair to the death of Louis XI.

It will be expedient, in view of the dissertation before us, to glance at the political relations of the states of Europe in the twelfth century. "There were certain great bundles of states connected by a dynastic or by a national unity—the Kingdom of France, the Empire of Germany, the Christian States of Spain . . . the still solid remnant of the Byzantine Empire, the well-compacted dominions of the Normans in Apulia and Sicily. Of these states, France, Germany and Spain were busily striving for consolida-

---

opposition down to a late day. This testamentary character of the French crown is a point that has not been enough emphasized.

In the encyclical letter of Ivo of Chartres (H. F., XV., 144) announcing the coronation of Louis VI. notice is taken of a complaint in Flanders that the doctrine of election had been violated. On the dangers incurred by the monarchy at the accession of Louis VI. owing to the coalition of the barons in favor of a pretender, see Luchaire, *Inst. Mon.*, I., p. 82–3, and notes. Orderic Vitalis (Book XIII., c. 12) notices the discontent of some of the barons, and clergy even, owing to the association of Louis VII. with his father.

[1] *Cf.* Stubbs, *Const. Hist. of England*, I., 187, where the opposite process is noticed of England.

tion or against dissolution. . . . Constantinople was far removed
from the interests of Christendom; her face set always eastward
in church and state. The Norman state in Apulia and Sicily was
the best organized and most united kingdom, and this taken in
conjunction with the wealth, splendor, ability and maritime
superiority of the kings, gave it an importance much greater than
was due to its extent. All the great powers, with the exception
of the last, had their energies for the most part employed in
domestic struggles, and were prevented by the interposition of small
semi-neutral countries from any extensive or critical collision,
whilst much of their naturally aggressive spirit was carried off to
the east. Between the Normans and the *de facto* empire lay the
debatable and unmanageable estates of the papacy, and the bulwark of Lombardy, itself a task for the whole imperial energies
of the empire. Between the same empire and France lay the
remains of the ancient Lotharingian and Burgundian kingdoms,
from the North Sea to the Mediterranean, hardly even more than
nominally imperial — a region destined to be the battle ground
of many generations as soon as the rival nations should have consol-
idated themselves and girt up their strength. But at present by
broad intervening barriers and by constant occupation at home,
now in the humiliation of aspiring vassals, now in the struggle for
existence against the overwhelming power of the greater feudatories, now in the maintenance of peace between rivals, the two
great representatives of the resurrection of European life, the
Kingdoms of France and Germany were kept at arms' length from
each other."[1] Thus in the twelfth century no two states of
Europe were in immediate contact or immediate rivalry save
France and England, an exception which was owing to the accident of the Norman Conquest.

Such is a general view of the political condition of Europe in
the twelfth century. What of the manner of life of the men of
that time? Gaul in the early twelfth century was a land divided
by differences of race not yet amalgamated; by differences
of rule, which were the pretext of endless wars; by grow-

[1] Stubbs. The "wonderful preface" to Roger of Hoveden. II. LXX–I.
(Rolls Series.)

ing differences of faith even—true forerunners of the Reformation. The land was dotted with feudal castles, the abbeys were veritable fortresses. Riot and ruin prevailed beyond the pale of the castle ; the country was sparsely populated. Agriculture was nearly impossible save in the narrow circle which the towns might protect, or in the breadth of land which some baron of more than ordinary power and insight might make secure. It was an iron age, when one must be either hammer or anvil. Life was rude and full of energy, because its vigorous requirements killed feeble organisms. But sometimes these iron men were of fine temper. The century that cast up in France such a ruffian as Thomas de Marle also brought St. Bernard and Abelard to light.

In such a time did Louis VI. of France, the first ruler of the Capetian house to make the theories of the monarchy active sources of power, come to the throne which his father had humiliated and dishonored. Public authority was dissolved, law defied, confusion reigned. The state needed a man of power to arrest dissolution, to restore law and to rebuild public authority. Like Edward I. he might be a man of constructive genius ; like Cromwell or Cavour, he might believe in some great militant principle; he must accept existing conditions and know how to turn them to best account. Such a man was Louis VI. of France. He was neither theorist nor fanatic. He knew how to build because he knew how to select the elements of strength that still survived in the midst of the surrounding confusion and use them to the best advantage.

The new Capetian monarchy in spite of its promise and its prediction had hitherto failed. The king was supposed to be the personification of justice.[1] As chief of the kingdom he was charged with the defense of the realm.[2] The peace of the church and the protection of the feeble and oppressed were his to maintain.[3] These duties, with the possible exception of King Hugh, no Capetian had yet fulfilled. The crown which Philip

[1] Dedecet enim regem transgredi legem, cum et rex et lex eandem imperandi excipiant majestatem.—Suger, 50.

[2] Brussel, I., 693, 868.

[3] Luchaire, *Manuel*, § § 250, 460.

left to his noble son was thus far from being a kingly one. The realm was small.[1] The royal power was lean and emaciated,[2] and the name king itself sullied and tarnished.

Louis, owing to the weakness and mismanagement had scarcely any tangible basis upon which to rest his authority. In the sphere of direct influence he was confined almost entirely[3] to the Ile-de-France, and even here the barons were accustomed to defy the crown and do much as they pleased.[4] And yet through the steady application of an authority at first merely nominal, he constructed at last a compacted political organism[5]

---

[1] The duchy of France which was the kernel of the kingdom, was reduced, as nearly as can be ascertained, to the Ile-de-France, l'Orléanais, the French Vexin, Bourges with the neighboring estates, and the chattelany of Dun-le-Roi. (Luchaire, *Inst. Mon.*, II., 298.) But any absolute statement of the extent of the realm at this time is impossible, as the crown possessed scattered holdings outside of what has generally been considered the royal domain. "The former view that the domain was a compact and circumscribed entity, like the duchy of Normandy, has been abandoned in the face of evidence that, beside the two hereditary territories of the Capetians, . . . the monarchy possessed various scattered holdings in territories outside of what has usually been considered the royal domain."—Walker, 118 and note 1. *Cf.* Luchaire, *Inst. Mon.*, I., 89. According to Gaillard, I. 185, the royal domain, at this time, did not constitute one-twentieth of the present France.

For the territorial expansion of the crown under Philip I. see Luchaire, *Inst. Mon.* II., 246-8. On the purchase of Bourges, see *Continuator of Aimon*, H. F., XI., 157. Philip I. dreamed of real dominion south of the Loire. The importance of this acquisition is given by Brussel I., 149, 166, 401. Foulque Rechin ceded the Gâtinais to Philip I. in order to assure Philip's neutrality in his absence.—H. F., XI., 394.

[2] But the *theory* of royal authority still remained and even grew under the weaker kings: "Rien ne prouve mieux l'intensité du courant qui portait alors (under Philippe le Hardi) la France vers l'unité monarchique, que la force croissante de la royauté sous un roi faible."—Langlois, *Positions des thèses de l'École des Chartes*, 1885, p. 96. Published in book form under the title, *Le Règne de Philippe le Hardi*, Paris, 1887.

[3] The penetration of the authority of the crown into remote fiefs through the right of *regale* allowed the king a measure of authority not otherwise possible. On the *regale, in extenso*, see Phillips, *Ursprung des Regalienrechts in Frankreich*, Halle, 1870.

[4] Suger, passim.

[5] Monod, *Revue historique*, XLII., 373.

over which a genuine sovereignty prevailed. To him the royal power was the instrument of justice.[1] To him the king was the incarnate expression of the will of the state — the personification of its invisible majesty.[2] With these lofty conceptions of the royal dignity, Louis united the most intense activity.[3] He appreciated the finer advantages to be derived from legal and institutional changes, as the creation of the right of appeal, and the establishment of liege homage testify.[4]

Thus he enlisted to his support all forces, new and old, in government and society. He so centralized his power in the Ile-de-France that his successors henceforth enjoyed its undivided resources. It is significant that he added nothing to the territory of France until the very last year of his life. The increase of royal authority in extension was conditioned on the internal strengthening of the regulative power. Louis VI. was content to confine his energies within the limits of ancient Neustria. His intervention in Bourbonnais and Auvergne, and certain dealings in Flanders, Bourgogne and Languedoc are exceptional and isolated cases.[5] But within the limits prescribed, there was no particular jurisdiction over which he did not exercise an influence. The feudal aristocracy, the communes, even the church, felt the directive hand of the monarchy. With him

[1] Quia fortissima regum dextra offitii jure votivo, tirannorum audacia quotiens eos guerris lacessiri vident, infinite gratulantem rapere, pauperes confundere, ecclesias destruere, interpolata licencia quam si semper liceret, insanius inflammantur malignorum instar spirituum, qui quos timent perdere magis trucidant, quos sperent retinere omnino fovent, fomenta flammis apponunt ut infinite crudelius devorent.—Suger, 80-1.

[2] Dedecet enim regem transgredi legem, cum et rex et lex eandem imperandi excipiant majestatem.—Suger, 50.

[3] In den ersten Generationen dieses Hauses, vor Erwerbung der Krone, finden wir lauter tapfere und emporstrebende Naturen. Nach denen folgten andere, die, durch Sinnesweise und Lage friedfertig gestimmt, beinahe einen priesterlichen Charakter trugen, ihr Königthum war mehr eine Würde, als eine Macht; jetzt unter veranderten Umständen gehen Manner aus ihm hervor, welche den Schwung altgemeiner Ideen mit Thatkraft verbinden.—Ranke, *Werke*, VIII., 24.

[4] See this dissertation, pp. 39-43.

[5] Luchaire, *Inst. Mon.*, II., 284.

began the *intensive* development of the French monarchy.
Others had given France the crown. Louis VI. gave the kingship.[1] Others after him were to give the kingdom. It was
Louis VI. who made possible that extensive development which
characterized the reign of Philip Augustus, and the splendor of
the Capetian House as it shone forth under St. Louis and Philip
the Fair.

[1] Louis VI. avait donné à la couronne une suprématie féodale réele. Phillippe Auguste lui procura une force territoriale disproportionnée avec celle des
grands vassaux.—M. Mignet, *Mem. de l'Acad. des Sc. mor. et pol.*, VI., 709. *Cf.*
Luchaire, *Inst. Mon.*, II., 255.

CHAPTER I.

THE WAR OF THE VEXIN.

Louis, or Louis Thibaud, the sixth of that name to become king of France, was born, probably, in the latter part of the year 1081.[1] His father, Philip I., was deficient in energy and sunk in sensual indulgences. These traits of character the son inherited, in less degree, but they never were suffered to impair the energy of his intellect or will. The surname "the Fat "(*le Gros*), by which Louis VI. is known in history, is a stigma. Such a title was no misnomor with a monarch like Charles the Fat, who was lethargic and weak, but it is unjust for history so to designate one who in life was known by the far more appropriate *soubriquets* of "the Wide-Awake" (*l'Éveille*), and "the Warlike" (*le Battailleur*). His early education was received in the abbey of St. Denis, where he learned to know and appreciate the abilities of his humbler school-fellow, Suger, afterwards minister of the crown, regent of France, and the first great finance minister of whom she can boast.[2]

The period of the life of Louis until the war of the Vexin is not characterized by any special mention by the chronicles. He was then sixteen years of age.[3] The war was insignificant in political results.[4] It brought no practical good to the young Louis, save that it gave him training for the larger work of later years. The history of the struggle is valuable, however, in that

[1] Luchaire, *Annales*, No. 1.

[2] It is said that Suger was the first to perceive that the vulgar idiom might be employed with value in the royal chronicles. The fact is not established, but Suger at least merits a high place in the rôle of French historians.—Lacroix, *Science and Literature in the Middle Ages*, English trans., London, 1878, p. 468.

[3] Luchaire, *Annales*, No. 6.

[4] "It is a war which supplies no remarkable instances, personal or political."—Freeman, *Norman Conquest*, V., p. 101.

it shows clearly the weakness of France, the strength of the baronage, and gives promise of a national spirit, as yet unapprehended.

There had been a long-standing quarrel between France and Normandy which became of importance only towards the end of the Conqueror's reign.[1] While the general ground of hostility was Norman jealousy of the overlord at Paris, the established pretext was the question of supremacy over the French Vexin.[2] Norman historians claimed[3] that Henry of France had ceded the strip to Robert of Normandy in return for help of arms given by the latter, and that William the Conqueror had failed to claim it only on account of wider interests across the channel and in Maine.[4] Border warfare was, therefore, rife and the Conqueror at last determined to put a stop to the trouble by a peremptory demand for the disputed tract.[5] The result was the war in which he met his death. The conditions of his will brought peace for a time by the separation of England and Normandy. But when all Normandy fell to Rufus, a dream of continental empire filled his mind,[6] and England was forced again to become a partner in the interests at stake between France and the great barrier

[1] See Marion, *De Normannorum ducum cum Capetianis pacta ruptaque societate.* Paris, 1892.

[2] On the acquisition of the Vexin by Philip I. see Luchaire, *Inst. Mon.*, p. 247.

[3] Ord. Vit. III., 223.

[4] *Ibid.* The uncertain feudal relation of the Vexin was further aggravated by the conduct of the Count of the Vexin, who held a unique position half way between baronage and hierarchy, being alike a vassal and a patron of St. Denis, while in his style he pretended perfect independence.—*Brussel,* I., 542.

[5] Ord. Vit. III., 223.

[6] Dicebatur equidem vulgo regem illum superbum et impetuosum aspirare ad regnum Francorum.—Suger, p. 7.

Ord. Vit. IV., 80, is fuller: Maximam jussit classem præparari et ingentem equitatum de Anglia secum comitari, ut pelago transfretato, in armis ceu leo supra prædam præsto consisteret, fratrem ab introitu Neustriæ bello abigeret, Aquitaniæ ducatum pluribus argenti massis emeret, et obstantibus sibi bello subactis, usque ad Garumnam fluvium imperii sui fines dilataret.

It is to be remembered that the Aquitaine of those days lay north of the Garonne river; the Aquitaine of which Cæsar speaks is southern Aquitaine.

province. By gaining the Vexin Rufus would deprive France
of frontier protection,[1] and make way for further encroach-
ment.

But the English king had a very different person to deal with
from the unworthy Philip, who had opposed the conqueror.[2] In
1092 Philip had granted to his son Louis the rule of the Vexin,
with the towns of Mantes and Pontoise.[3] Five years later Rufus
made his demand of the French king, specifying Mantes, Chaumont and Pontoise,[4] and the war began in serious earnest.

The strength of William lay in the vast sums of money at his
disposal. The weakness of France lay in the venality and disloy-
alty of the border barons and in the impoverished condition of the
monarchy.[5] But to this was opposed the amazing energy of
Louis and the beginning of a French national sentiment. Suger
justifies his hero by the doctrine that it is not right or natural
that Frenchmen—he does not say France—be subject to Englishmen, or Englishmen to Frenchmen;[6] and even Ordericus Vitalis
could say of the brave men of the Vexin who fell in this war fight-

[1] Margiis regni collimitans.—Suger, 6.

[2] Louis le Gros was probably associated with his father on the throne in
1100 or 1101.—Luchaire, *Annales*, Appendix III. *Cf. Acad. des Inscrip.*, etc.,
IV., 489–508 (1805). Louis. when *rex designator*, used a seal which indicated
his martial character. In it he is represented clad in military habit, astride a
horse, with a lance in his right hand, in his left the reins. Mabillon, p. 594,
has a description of seal (1107) and on p. 427 is a picture of the seal. On the
position and influence of the crown prince, see Luchaire, *Inst. Mon.*, I.,
137–143.

[3] Ludovico filio suo consensu Francorum Pontisariam et Maduntum totumque
comitatum Vilcassinum donavit, totiusque regni curam, dum primo flore juven-
tutis pubesceret, commisit.—Ord. Vit. III., 390.

[4] Ord Vit., IV., 20. Suger, 6, states the fact without mentioning the fortresses. According to Palgrave (IV., 626) Rufus asserted a claim through his
mother Matilda to the Capetian crown, but as usual, he cites no authority for
the statement. Suger, 7, gives a different claim.

[5] Ille (Rufus) opulentus et Anglorum thesaurorum profusus mirabilisque
militum mercator et solidator; iste (Louis) deculii expers, patii qui benefitiis
regni utebatur parcendo, sola bone indolis industria militiam cogebat, audacter
resistebat.—Suger, 6.

[6] Nec fas nec naturale est Francos Anglis, immo Anglos Francis subici.—
Ibid., 7.

ing for their prince-count—*Seseque pro defensione patriæ et gloria gentis suæ, ad mortem usque inimicis objecerunt.*[1]

Louis had neither men nor money ; while Rufus was able to ransom English captives, Louis' prisoners had no hope of deliverance save in sacrificing honor for liberty and taking oath to fight against their natural overlord.[2] To the venality of the border baronage William addressed himself directly. The strategic situation of the castles of many of these petty lords made their allegiance of importance to either side. Of these, Guy-of-the-Rock, the lord of La Roche Guyon, was the most notorious.[3]

Count Robert of Meulan, whose fortress was further up the Seine, was another who for gold made a straight path for the English king into France.[4] Louis' energy, for one so young, is astonishing. He went far to the south for support. He drew on Berry, Burgundy and even Auvergne for knights,[5] and at last, although he had as often to flee as to fight,[6] he brought the Red King to a stand. William had dreamed of an Anglican conquest of France, but in spite of the aid of so formidable an ally as

[1] Ord. Vit., IV., 24.

[2] Verum Anglie captos redempcionem celerum militaris stipendii acceleravit anxietas, Francorum vero longa diuturni carceris maceravit prolixitas, nec ullo modo evinculari potuerunt, donec, suscepta ejusdem regis Anglie militia, hominio obligati, regnum et regem impugnare et turbare jurejurando firmaverunt.—Suger, 7.

[3] Suger describes the rock, chap. xvi. See Freeman's *William Rufus*, II., 180-1.

[4] Robertus itaque, comes de Mellento in suis munitionibus Anglos suscepit, et patentem eis in Galliam discursum aperuit.—Ord. Vit., IV., 21. In all this treachery, one baron, whom no price could buy, deserves to be mentioned. Helias of St. Sidoine. His castle of Bures on the Dieppe or Arques River was an effectual bar to Rufus' scheme of cutting off England and the Gifford barony. Rufus at last captured the castle, and so highly did he think of his capture that he transported the whole garrison to England. One is glad to know, however, that Helias himself escaped. Palgrave, IV., 405.

[5] Videres juvenem celerrimum modo Bituricensium, modo Alvernorum, modo Burgundiorum militari manu transvolare fines nec idcirco tardius, si ei ignotescat, Vilcassinum regredi, et cum trecentis aut quingentis militibus fortissime refragari, et ut dubius se habet belli eventus, modo cedere, modo fugare.—Suger, 6.

[6] *Supra.*

William of Aquitaine,[1] he could not wrest away the Vexin. A truce was made (1098) which was turned into a real peace by his death two years later, and the dream of an Anglican conquest slumbered for two centuries.[2]

[1] Ord. Vit., IV., 25.

[2] Velly (t. iii., 40) makes this war the beginning of the national rivalry of France and England. It began in the end of the year 1097, was waged most intensely in September, 1098, and ended with William's return to England in 1099.—Luchaire, *Annales*, Introd., xxxvii., ff; *Cf.* No. 6.

A full account of the war will be found in Freeman's *William Rufus*, II., 171–90. Gaillard, *Histoire de la Rivalité de la France et de l'Angleterre*, t. I., part I., chap. 3.

CHAPTER II.

THE LIBERATION OF THE REALM.

The War of the Vexin Louis fought as Crown Prince. Shortly after the peace, by the consent of the barons he was associated with his father on the throne.[1] In 1108 Philip died and Louis at once and without any serious protest[2] assumed the full direction of the monarchy.[3] The problem before him was synthetic — to unite in the kingship all the scattered elements of sovereignty diffused throughout the feudal state.[4] The feudal régime had reached its apogee. The monarchy retained hardly more than the ascription of authority.[5] The greater portion of the barons were not attached to the king by any precise homage or vigorous loyalty. The quasi-sovereignty of the dukes and counts formed a wall between their vassals and the king, and there was, therefore, no point of contact between the monarchy and seigneurs of the second degree.[6] Even under Philip Augustus the royal right to enter a fief not held immediately of the crown was precarious.[7]

[1] Luchaire, *Annales*, No. 8.

[2] In the encyclical letter of Ivo of Chartres, H. F., XV., 144, notice is taken of a slight discontent.

[3] Luchaire, *Annales*, No. 57.

[4] "L'histoire de France c'est l'histoire de la conquête de la France par la royauté, la substitution de l'unité à la variété féodale, de la centralisation à fédération."—M. Gabriel Monod, *Revue hist.*, Sept.–Oct. 1893, p. 101.

[5] Luchaire, *Manuel*, 243.

[6] *Inst. Mon.*, II., 29. On the general subject see *Ibid.* II., 21–36.

[7] Luchaire, *Manuel*, 257 ; Walker, 109. In the first article of the joint constitution (1209 or 1210) between Philip Augustus and the grand barons of the realm the difference between direct and rear vassals is clearly given :—Quicquid tenetur de domino ligie, vel alio modo, si contigerit per successionem heredum vel quocunque alio modo divisionem inde fieri, quocunque modo fiat, omnes qui de feodo illo tenebunt, de domino feodo *principaliter* et *nullo modo* tenebunt, sicut unus antea tenebat priusquam divisio esset facta.—(Brussel, I.,

The relation of the great lords to their vassals was almost similar in kind to that which the barons themselves sustained towards
the king. Even fiefs of the church enjoyed such high authority.
The political power of certain ecclesiastical dignitaries exceeded
even their spiritual authority, as in the case of Stephen de
Garland.[1]

The social and economic condition was as bad as the political.
In order that he might save expense, many a baron neglected to
repair the roads which sank into quagmires ; river channels would
become obstructed by sand-bars ; bridges be swept away and not
rebuilt. The barriers which feudal usurpations opposed to commerce were interminable. The number and kind of exactions
were very many. Each petty baron demanded toll for the use of
road, bridge, or ferry, while strangers were regarded as legitimate
objects of extortion.[2] Often the guard of protection was a band
of brigands. The seigneur found it a lucrative practice to plunder merchants and wayfarers. Gregory VII. had accused Philip
I. of despoiling Italian merchants who resorted to the fairs in
France.[3]

This was the sort of men control of whom was laid upon the
shoulders of the young king. No wonder he was in continual
war.[4] The territory of the enemy began a few miles from Paris ;

15). The grand fiefs were duchies and counties; after them came chatellanies
(*Ibid.*, I., 173). A viscounty and a chatellany were one and the same thing
(*Ibid.*, II., 676-7). Many hereditary viscounties in the twelfth century consisted
of a *château* or fortified *ville* with a considerable domain, together with the serfs
and appurtenances upon it. On this process of feudalization see Brussel, I., 44, ff.

[1] See this dissertation, pp. 48 ff. The bishops of Laon, Châlons and Beauvais were also great lay lords. Pfister, *Le Règne de Robert le Pieux*, 184.

[2] " Ces impôts, qui nous paraissent si étranges par leur multiplicité et par
leur noms que nous ne comprenons plus, étaient au fond aussi legitimes et
aussi conformes à toute l'organisation sociale que nos impôts actuels. La
féodalité était une gendarmerie."—Pigeonneau, I., 99.

[3] Epistolae, September 1074, to the French clergy; and to William of Poitiers, November 1076.—H. F., XIV., 583, 587. See the canons of the councils
of Clermont (1130), Rheims (1131), etc. Praecipimus ut . . . . peregrini et
mercatores et rustici euntes et redeuntes . . . . omni tempore securi sunt.—
Canon of Clermont, 8.

[4] In marte continuo — Suger, 35.

the king could not go from his capital to Orléans or Compiègne
without a band of men-at-arms.[1] The moral advantage of royalty,
though not so slight as sometimes supposed,[2] had little influence
over a horde of lusty barons who fattened on war and had
nothing to gain from peace;[3] whose delight was to exercise "the
sovereign rights of slaughter and havoc;" to whom glory was
physical prowess; the baseness of whose life was relieved only by
the faint demands of chivalry.[4]

Louis, however, was not without some advantages in the
struggle. The age in which he lived was not unfavorable for a
man who knew how to make the most of what it afforded. The
eleventh century had closed with the first crusade and the conquest of the Holy Land. The twelfth century began with Abelard and the communal movement—the two liberties essential
to constitutional life—liberty of the spirit and civil liberty.[5]
With that pious crusading enthusiasm which led men to sell
their own lands in order to see others, Louis had little sympathy,
but he was quick enough to see the good results likely to accrue
to the throne from the absence of turbulent vassals in the East.[6]
Two classes, the bourgeoisie and the lower clergy, whose spirit of
subordination resulting from the hierarchical organization, had
made them, on the whole, favorable to authority, were equally
devoted to the king.[7] In fact the church generally was faithful

[1] Cumque a fluvio Sequano Corbeilo, medio vie Monte Leherii, a dextra
Castella Forti pagus Parisiacus circumcingentur, inter Parisienses et Aurelianses
tantum confusionis chaos firmatum erat, ut neque hi ad illos neque illi ad istos
absque perfidorum arbitrio nisi in manu forti valerent transmeare.—Suger, 19.

[2] Luchaire, Inst. Mon., I., 54.

[3] Pace nihil luctrantes.—Suger, 80.

[4] Freeman, William Rufus, II., Appendix I. The conduct of Henry I. of
England towards Louis VI. in the battle of Bremule illustrates the prevalence
of chivalric ideas.—Suger, 91-2.

[5] Gebhart, Les Origines de en Renaissance en Italie, Paris, 1878, p. 28.

[6] The notorious Hugh de Puiset went to the Holy Land (1128) and thus
rid France of one of the most despicable and dangerous of cut-throats. He
founded the dynasty of the Counts of Jaffa.—Suger, 79, n. 5. Gui Troussel and the Count of Rochefort were in the First Crusade.—Ibid., 18, 19 and
n. 4.

[7] Combes, 132.

to the interests of monarchy. The *Truce of God* promulgated at
the council of Clermont (1095) had been an effort to regulate the
disordered condition of affairs.[1]   The church which had retained
the most unity in the prevailing dismemberment of political
society had sought to remedy the evils of robbery, plunder, ship-
wrecking[2] and private war,[3] not as formerly, by hurling anathemas, but by virtually instituting home crusades on the part of
the clergy.   The property of the church repleted the insufficient
revenues of the king; the church supplied the emasculated monarchy with men.[4]

The imminence of the danger from the violence of the barons
had produced a salutary bestirring in royal circles towards the
end of Philip's reign.   We are not to think that Philip was as
incapable as is commonly supposed.[5]   He was inert; still he had,
at least, the merit of feeling the need of restoring the monarchy
to power and of appreciating the valuable abilities of his son, to
whom the credit of this movement was largely due.   The will to
accomplish his purpose, however, the father lacked.

The field of Louis' action was in the main confined to the
spaces between the five cities of Paris, Orléans, Étampes, Melun
and Compiègne;[6] all the intermediate territory was occupied by

[1] See Ivo of Chartres, epist. 90 (H. F., XV., 110) for an elucidation of the
character and scope of the Truce of God.   The oath is given in Rod. Glab.,
IV., c. 5, V. c. 1.   The restrictions largely failed of their purpose owing to
being too stringent for the times (DuCange, *Treva*).

[2] This was prohibited by Philip Augustus.—Walker, 103.

[3] For the efforts of the Carlovingians to regulate private war, see Beth-
mann-Hollweg, *Civilprozess*, I., 464–5.   For its prevalence in the eleventh
and twelfth centuries, see *Mon. Germ. Hist. Scriptores*, XV., 839, 858, 879,
1146, and DuCange. Dissert., XXIX.—M. Rambaud (*Civilisation française*,
5th edit., 1893, Vol. I., p. 224), says that Louis IX., in establishing the
Quarantaine-le-roi, simply revived an ordinance of Louis VI.

[4] Ludovicus. . . . auxilium per Galliam deposcere coactus est episcoporum.
Tunc ergo communitas in Francia popularis statuta est a praesulibus, ut
presbyteri comitarentur regi ad obsidionem vel pugnam cum vexillis et
parochianis omnibus.—Ord. Vit., IV., 285, Suger, 65, says — cum communitates
patriae parochiorum adessent.

[5] Luchaire, *Inst. Mon.*, II., 241.

[6] Sismondi, V., 86.

barons who, fortified in their *châteaux*, made "a thievish living on the common road." The danger from the barons was so great that even upon the death of Philip I. Louis VI. had himself crowned at Orleans by the archbishop of Sens instead of at Rheims, the usual place of coronation.[1] The conflict was fierce and unremitting, and Louis displayed prodigious courage. He was always in the forefront urging his men by word and deed. In the siege of the Chateau de Mouchi his ardor carried him into the keep, although the castle was a mass of flames. He escaped, but lost the use of his voice for months to come.[2] In the autumn of 1107, in the campaign against Humbaud of Sainte-Severe-sur-Indre, when the king's men had to cross that river in the face of the foe, Louis set an example by leaping into the water and fording the stream, although it was up to the barred front of his helmet.[3]

It would be profitless to give a detailed account of these campaigns;[4] but certain salient features are to be observed:

First, every fortress taken was leveled, or else entrusted to parties of assured fidelity.[5]

Second, some castles were too strong to be taken by arms, but the possession of them was of vital importance to Louis'

[1] Si consecratio regis differetur, writes Ives de Chartres, regni status et ecclesiae pax graviter periclitaretur. (H. F., XV., 144. *Cf.* Suger, 39–41.) Moreover, the archbishop of Rheims had just been elected and had not yet taken his seat. Luchaire, *Inst. Mon.*, I., 70, and note 3. *Cf.* Luchaire, *Inst. Mon.*, I., 82–3.

[2] Tanta viri erat animositas, ut nec incendium declinare curaret cum et ei et exercitui periculosum esset et multo tempore maximam ei raucitatem generaret.—Suger, 10.

[3] See the spirited account in Suger, c. xi. On this expedition into Bourbonnais see M. Brial's analytical memoir in the *Acad. des Inscript.*, VI. (1824), pp. 129-137.

[4] Sixteen are recorded by Suger alone.

[5] Louis VI. was the first to forbid the erection of fortresses in the Ile-de-France without the consent of the king.—Brussel, I., 381. He constructed walls in the vicinity of Paris, erected fortresses and placed towers upon the bridges to facilitate the defense of the city.—Dulaure, *Hist. de Paris.* Paris, 1829 (fourth edition), Vol. II., p. 46. See the *Notitia de Constructione castri Karoli-Vanae*, H. F., XIV., 221, Luchaire, *Annales*, No. 324.

scheme of consolidation. There were two of these, whose loca-
tion was such as to make their occupation by the king imperative.
They were the Château of Montlhery, and that of La Roche
Guyon.[1] They were impregnable, and a constant menace. The
first was situated, in the striking words of Suger, in the very
vitals of the kingdom.[2] So essential[3] was the adherence of its
lord that King Philip (we may believe at the instance of Louis,)
offered his natural son Philip in marriage to Guy's[4] daughter
Elizabeth, who brought with her Montlhery as dowry. Louis,
on his part, ceded to his half-brother the castle of Mantes as a
mark of confidence. But Philip repaid the confidence by
intriguing with Amauri IV. de Montfort, Foulque V. the Young
of Anjou,[5] and the mother of Philip, Bertrade, the king's
mistress and late Countess of Anjou.[6] In order to secure La
Roche Guyon Louis himself espoused Lucienne, the daughter of
Guy of the Rock.[7]

Third, Louis gave active support to the great prelates of the
realm. In 1102 or 1103 he succored the church of Rheims,
harried by Ebles II., Count de Roucy,[8] and the year afterwards
petition came for help from the sanctuary of Orleans.[9] Nothing
could more plainly evince the boldness of the barons. The

[1] La Roche Guyon is described in Freeman's *William Rufus*, II., 180–1.

[2] In ipsis regni visceribus.—Suger, 57.

[3] Valde enim appetebant castrum. *Ibid.*, 18.

[4] Qua occasione castri custodie sue recepto, tamquam si oculo suo festucam eruissent aut circumsepti repagula dirupissent, exhilarescunt.—*Ibid.* Gui Troussel was a son of Milon I. of Montlhery.—Suger, 18, n. 1.

[5] Suger, 57.

[6] For the machinations of Bertrade, see Ord. Vit., IV., 195 ff., and Free-man's *William Rufus*, II., 173–4.

[7] This marriage was dissolved at the Council of Troyes in 1107. Luchaire, *Inst. Mon.*, I., 182, attributes the rupture with the family of Rochefort to the plottings of the Garlands. (Cf. Suger, 19, n. 5). The Count of Rochefort was seneschal in 1091, and was replaced by Payen de Garland at the time of the First Crusade. On Guy's return from the Holy Land (about 1104) he was rein-stalled in the office. But the ascendancy of the Garlands acquired during his absence, created jealousy and finally open rupture between him and the king. (*Ibid.*, 18, n. 4.)

[8] Suger, 14.

[9] *Ibid.*, 15.

archbishop of Rheims was grand chancellor of the realm,[1] while the church of Orleans had been for generations under the special protection of the crown, and, next to Rheims, was the most noted cathedral west of the Rhine.

Fourth, as Louis' power grew, the sphere of application enlarged. The barons were to learn, as Suger aptly said, that "kings have long arms."[2] In 1115, Alard Guillebaud, of Berry, solicited the king's help in recovering the seigneury usurped by his uncle, Aimond Vairevache, of Bourbon.[3] Louis lost no time. The way to the south was open. Not since the days of Robert the Pious had a French monarch been so far from his capital.[4] But a grander opportunity for the extension of royal power to the south was at hand. The bishop of Clermont had complained of the Count of Auvergne in 1121 (?).[5] Five years later another expedition was necessary.[6] But the count was a vassal of the great duke of Aquitaine,[7] the most powerful lord in the south. Interference by the king with a rear vassal was a thing hitherto unheard of in feudal law. But the king was strong. He had with him Charles the Good of Flanders, Foulque of Anjou, and the Count of Brittany, besides many barons of the realm.[8] Thus surrounded by what was in fact his *curia regis*, Louis entered

[1] Luchaire, *Inst. Mon.*, I., 188 ; Mabillon, 113.

[2] Suger, 83, quoting Ovid, Heroides, XVII., 166. Scitur enim longas regibus esse manus.

[3] *Ibid.*, c. xxiv. This was between 1108–15. See Luchaire, *Annales*, Nos. 91–2. *Acad. des Inscrip.*, etc., VII., 129 (1806). *Cf.* Guizot, IV., 120–2.

[4] Pfister, *Le Règne de Robert le Pieux*, 286, 294.

In 1134 Louis VI. granted to Humbert, bishop of Puy-en-Velay, the exercise of regalian rights in the absence of his lord, the Count of Tripoli, in Syria. Luchaire, *Annales*, 532. According to Sismondi (V. 255) this is the first appearance of royal authority so far south in one hundred and twenty-four years.

[5] Suger, 108 and n. 1.

[6] On the dates of these expeditions, see Suger, 108, nn. 1, 3, 4, and Luchaire *Annales* No. 369.

[7] Suger, 109.

[8] Erant in ejus expedicione, comes prepotens Flanderensis Karolus, comes Andegavensis Fulco, comes Brittanie, tributarius regis anglici Henrici de Normannia exercitus, barones et regni optimates.—*Ibid.*, 108.

Auvergne, gave judgment and made execution.[1] The Count of Auvergne called upon his suzerain. Duke William came with his army, but when he saw the host of the king he was filled with fear and admiration. He did homage to Louis VI., and acknowledged the royal right to take cognizance of the indirect vassals of the crown.[2] *Arrière-ban* had been delivered a telling blow. The precedent was not forgotten, although it took years of patient persistence for the crown entirely to establish the new right.[3]

Finally, it is to be noticed that the history of these wars has an intimate connection with the *curia regis*, and therefore has a direct relation to the general history of France and the progress of royal power. The king had a triple mission; he was legislator, judge and sheriff, all in one.[4] The administration of justice was in a sorry state when Louis, as prince, assumed active direction.[5] These campaigns were in reality executions of judgments,[6] often by default. They were preceded by a court pro-

---

[1] Rex cum optimatibus regni consulens.—*Ibid.*, 110. At the end of the reign of Philip the charters distinguished between ordinary counsellors (*curiales*) and the greater feudal advisers (*fideles* or *optimates*). It is stretching the text, however, to see in this allusion of Suger the peers of later France.—Suger, 110, n. 1. What we have is the *curia regis*, still as an ambulatory body. See this dissertation p. 41-2.

[2] Suger, 109–110. The speech of Duke William is very significant : "Dux tuus Aquitanie, domine rex, multa te salute, omni te potui honore. Non dedignetur regie majestatis celsitudo ducis Aquitanie servitium suscipere, jus suum ei conservare, quia sicut justicia exigit servitium, sic et justum exigit dominium. Arvernensis comes, quia Alvernian a me, quam ego a vobis habeo, si quid commisit curie vestre vestro habeo imperio representare. Hoc nunquam prohibuimus, hoc etiam modo offerimus et ut suscipiatis suppliciter efflagitamus. Et ne super his celsitudo vestra dubitare dignetur, multos sufficientes obsides dare paratos habemus. Si sic indicaverint regni optimates, fiat, sin aliter, sicut."

[3] This fellowship is the beginning of the friendly relations of France and Aquitaine, which culminated in the union of Louis the Young and Eleanor. Louis VII. sustained the right of intervention in Auvergne. *Hist. du Roi Louis VII.*, c. xxii. ; Luchaire, *Inst. Mon.*, II., 293.

[4] Luchaire, *Inst. Mon.*, I., vii. Pardessus, 25–6.

[5] Ludovicus itaque . . . . illuster et animosus regni paterni defensor ecclesiarum utilitatibus providebat; oratorum (aratorum?), laboratorum et pauperum quod diu insolitum fuerat, quieti studebat.—Suger, 9.

[6] Brussel, I., 326.

cess, although such process was little more than a matter of form in the case of such bandits as Thomas de Marle[1] and Hugh of Puiset.[2] It was a maxim of feudal law that no arrest could take place in the court itself.[3] However great the annoyances were in his long struggle with the feudality, Louis had always an instinctive reverence for law.[4] He respected the rules of feudal law — what Suger styles the " custom of the French "[5] or the " Salic law."[6] The principle and interests of the monarchy demanded a legal basis to operate upon.   Louis made his judgments hard because he believed that if the king were lightly thought of in a case of little moment there would be no hope of justice in those involving large interests.[7] To that end he was always on the alert, summoning or executing in person or by agent, hearing causes of immediate instance as well as of appeal[8] and reversing lower decrees, if necessary.[9]

This consideration leads to an inquiry into the judicial system of the Capetian monarchy.

[1] For Thomas de Marle and his brigandages consult Guibert de Nogent, III., c. xi.

[2] For those of Hugh de Puiset, see Suger, cc. xviii., xxi.

[3] Non tentus, neque enim Francorum mos est.—Suger, 9.

[4] See this dissertation, introd. p. 9.

[5] Francorum mos est, etc.—Suger, 9.

[6] *Ibid.*, 37. Suger uses some queer expressions to define feudal relations. Thus (p. 35) Theobald is "non eminus sed comminus." The author of the *Chroniques de Saint Denis*, III., 245, interprets this thus : "Eut le sire du règne fait mander son arrière-ban et les gens voisines semonses, car il n'eut pas loisir de mander loing souldoiers."—Suger, 35, n. 3. Again (p. 107) Suger speaks of Foulque of Anjou, Conan of Brittany and the Counts of Nevers and Berry as "regni debitores," meaning grand vassals. He is in error regarding the last two.

[7] Louis VI. writes to Calixtus II., Rex ergo Franciae, qui proprius est Romanæ ecclesiæ filius, si in facili causa, si in levi petitione contemnitur, nulla spes in majori relinquitur.—H. F. XV., 340.

[8] On appeal see this dissertation, pp. 39–41.

[9] He sends word to Thierry of Flanders (1132) to look after the bishop of Arras, Alvisus, whom Eustace de la Longue had wronged by a false decree,— contra justitiam et rationem in curia sua. H. F., XV., 342–3. See Luchaire, *Inst. Mon.*, I., 300–1. Langlois, *Textes relatifs à l'Histoire du Parlement,* No. VII.

CHAPTER III.

THE COURT OF THE KING AND ITS JUDICIAL FUNCTIONS UNDER LOUIS VI.[1]

ORGANIZATION — EXTENSION OF ITS COMPETENCE — CHANGES IN FEUDAL LAW.

The highest court of justice was a bench composed of the princes of the blood, the grand vassals of the crown, seigneurs holding immediately of the king, archbishops, bishops and the officers of the king's palace.[2] It was commonly called the *curia regis*.[3] The participation of the vassals was more or less complete according to circumstances.[4] The ordinance therein made with the consent of the baronage, was less an act of the express will of the suzerain than a political agreement. It was sanctioned by a greater or less number of vassals, as the case was, and was executory throughout the extent of the realm.[5] As far as they contributed to the making of the law, the signing barons engaged for and against all, to put it into execution. They were

---

[1] See Luchaire, *La Cour du Roi et ses fonctions judiciaires sous le règne de Louis VI.*

[2] *Cf.* H. F., X., 627, XI. 407.

[3] Comes quidam malefactor, nomine Rodolphus, qui res ecclesiæ per injustam occasionem invaserat . . . appelatus fuit in Curia Regis.—Letter of Fulbert of Chartres to John XIX., H. F., X., 473.

The common expressions employed to denote the royal assembly are *curia regis, conventus, concilium* and *colloquium*. Sometimes, when of an ecclesiastical phase, the terms *synodus* or *placitum* are employed. In general, the convention was composed of the most prominent feudal and church representatives: the *principes*, the *primates* and the *proceres regis, i. e.,* the bishops and nobles (*episcopi et optimates, episcopi et barones*).—Luchaire, *Manuel*, 494.

[4] Pardessus, 29.

[5] Practically, the application of the law was much less than this. Even in the time of Philip Augustus these agreements "were no further binding than the personal territories of the contracting parties extended."—Walker, 68.

supposed to advise those vassals who were not present, and constrain those who did not wish to conform to the decree.[1]   In fact, it was sometimes specified that the signers had taken oath to enforce observation of the law upon all who essayed to infringe it.[2]   The competence of the court was thus very largely measured by the competence of the lords and councilors around the person of the king.[3]   The ecclesiastical seigneurs, being more dependent upon royalty, came more often and in greater numbers than the laity, and exercised a considerable influence over affairs pertaining to the baronage.   The reciprocal relation existing between the throne and the clergy, and the double power, feudal and ecclesiastical, of the latter, explains the importance of the clergy to the royal government.[4]   The church possessed the degree of instruction necessary to settle the difficulties over which the court of the king had jurisdiction.[5]   The ecclesiastics of Sens and Rheims, in whose jurisdiction lay the greater part of the lands immediately under royal authority, appear most frequently in the royal assembly.[6]   Among lay lords are first those not far removed from Paris, the small barons of Parisis, Vexin, Étampes, L'Orléanais, Beauvaisais, etc.; among high feudatories come the counts of Flanders, Ponthieu, Vermandois, Champagne, Nevers and Blois.[7]   As for the more distant feudal chiefs, their presence depended on the most diverse circumstances : geographical situation, or the more or less amicable relations with the crown being the principal determinants.   Before the twelfth century, the dukes of Normandy, Aquitaine and Burgundy, and the counts of Brittany, Anjou and Auvergne were present more

[1] Pardessus, 32.

[2] Luchaire, *Manuel*, 251–2.

[3] *Ibid.*, 557.

[4] Luchaire, *Inst. Mon.*, I., 294.

[5] Luchaire, *Manuel*, 494.

[6] Luchaire, *Manuel*, 495.

[7] It will be observed that the distinction which prevailed by the time of Philip Augustus, between the *regium concilium* and the *curia regis* cannot be ascertained at this time.   See Luchaire, *La Cour du Roi et ses fonctions judiciaires sous le règne de Louis VI.*, pp. 24–5.   *Cf.* Froidevaux, *De regiis conciliis Philippo II., Augusto regnante, habitis.*   Paris, 1891.

frequently than in the reign of Louis VI., when royalty was isolating itself in order to fortify and concentrate its powers.[1]

The court in the time of Louis VI. had cognizance of civil and criminal matters,[2] cases involving the communes,[3] appeals for redress or protection, and even such trivial things as a squabble between monks of rival monasteries.[4] The way in which Louis

[1] There is a distinction made in the feudal law of the tenth and eleventh centuries between the right of justice of the king as suzerain, and the right of justice of the king as prince of those who owe him fealty. In the latter case, the king sits less as a feudal lord than as a prince clothed with sovereignty, although the distinction lost its practical importance owing to the conduct of the kings. The *curia regis* originally comprised all *fideles* whom the king chose to summon. According to custom, unless it were a cause involving an ecclesiastical seigneur or a superior baron, one who was, therefore, not amenable to the judgment of simple vassals, the case was tried before the court of justice made up of ordinary vassals, *i. e.,* contests between vassals properly so-called were decided by a feudal court where they alone sat, which was merely an incorporation in the feudal régime of a principle which far antedated the existence of a feudal polity. But the fact that the king was also Duke of Francia made it possible for him to bring to bear a degree of authority upon the *fideles* which, while technically legal, tended to eliminate any action of theirs calculated to dominate in the *curia regis.* The vassals of the duke were necessarily also direct vassals of the king. The king caused the affairs even of *fideles* to be judged through the court of his own vassals, a method of procedure as effective as it was legitimate; for it was to royal advantage so to do, inasmuch as the constituency of the court was composed of the men who lived in his immediate neighborhood, and who were more likely to be under his control, as the grand officers of the crown, the seneschal, butler, chamberlain, constable and chancellor. The result was that by the twelfth century the *curia regis* had become, in principle, royal rather than feudal. The *curia regis* thus became technically a court of peers without being so in fact; a court whose competence no one could deny, but which was in fact a mixed court, which aided the king to transform his feudal suzerainty into sovereignty and rendered his sovereignty effective under the guise of a feudal suzerainty. See on this head, Flach, I., livre II., ch. viii., especially pp. 244–254; Heeren, *Pol. Werke,* II., 166 ff.

[2] Galbert de Bruges, c. 47.

[3] Langlois, *Textes relatifs à l'Hist. du Parlement,* No. VIII. Luchaire, *Manuel,* 557, c. On the capacity, in general, of the court, see Luchaire, *Inst. Mon.,* I., 289, ff.

[4] H. F., XIV., 156. The king released the monasteries from the jurisdiction of intermediate judges, allowing cases to come directly before him.— Brussel, I., 507.

insisted upon the competence of the royal court over the clergy
was dignified and steadfast.   Fortunately his two ministers,
Stephen de Garland, and after him Suger, churchmen though
they were, were in perfect accord with the king in maintaining
the dependence of the clergy upon the royal authority.[1]   The
court was also, on occasion, a national parliament, as when the
Emperor Henry V. threatened France.   It then enjoyed a truly
political character.[2]

The fluid composition of the court in the eleventh, and even
in the early twelfth century, is discernible in its lack of specific
organization.   Its procedure was feudal,[3] with frequent recourse
to trial by battle.   Acts of general interest are rare.   Legislation
is accompanied by the use of grandiloquent phrases, as *edictum
regulis imperii, signum serenissimi ac gloriossismi regis, auctoritatis nostrae praeceptum*, and the like.[4]   The acts are disfigured
with interminable preambles, and encumbered with numerous
signatures.   Under Louis le Gros, however, they become more
formal and simple.   Instead of the inscriptions of a motley array
of court retainers, nobles, chaplains, physicians, tutors and even
cooks and scullions, who all took a hand in the business under

---

[1] See the complaint of Hildebert, archbishop of Tours (1126), writing probably to the papal legate.   H. F., XV., 319.   Louis VI. would not let decrees of
an ecclesiastical tribunal be valid till sanctioned by him.   "Dehinc auditu
utriusque partis causa, cum ego adhuc debitum expectarem judicium.   Rex mihi
per se ipsum prohibuit ne quidquam de praedictarum redditibus dignitatum aut
praesumerem aut ordinarem."   *Cf. Letter of Honorius II., Ibid.*, XV., 321.
Acquisition or alienation of fiefs by the church he made conditional on royal
consent.—"Non enim licet episcopo feodum aliquod sine nostro et capituli sui
assensu de rebus ecclesiae alicui prebere : quod profecto judicium et approbamus
et ubique in regno nostro ergo ecclesiae tenemus" (1132).—Langlois, *Textes
relatifs à l'Histoire du Parlement*, No. VII.   Consult Luchaire, *Inst. Mon.*, I.,
282-8 ; 294-300.   See also the elaborate case of the partition of the rights of
the banlieue with the Archbishop of Paris, Luchaire, *Annales*, No. 218
Luchaire, *La Cour du Roi et ses fonctions judiciaires sou* `'* règne de Louis VI.*,
pp. 17-18.   Guérard, *Cartul de Notre-Dame de Paris*, I., 252.   The act itself is
in Tardif, No. 345.

[2] Suger, 103.   Luchaire, *Inst. Mon.*, I., 267-8.

[3] Luchaire, *Manuel*, 558.

[4] Mabillon, 110.

the early kings, we find now such promiscuous attention to the
work of the *curia regis* increasingly rare; and sometimes only
the signatures of the seneschal, butler, chamberlain, constable
and chancellor.[1] A refreshing revival of ancient forms is also
noticeable, borrowed from the old Frankish chancery.[2] More
care is taken in chronology,[3] and the seal is more carefully
affixed.[4] Refusals to obey court summons also cease almost
entirely. The refractory barons protest and procrastinate, and
with one accord make excuses, but seldom refuse obedience to
the summons.[5]

The revival of the Carlovingian chancery suggests another
reform made by Louis le Gros, partaking somewhat of Carlovingian forms. Even towards the end of the eleventh century
may be discerned that contraction in the constituency of the
curia regis which gave rise to the institution of the *palatins*, an
administrative body of preponderant authority in the next century.[6] This change is a sure sign of centralization. Gradually
the king, about whose person the palatins habitually gathered,
came to entrust to them, as the exigency arose, duties of an
administrative nature, judicial inquiries, or diplomatic errands.[7]

[1] In the session of the court under Philip I. (1066) an act is signed by
twenty-four persons (Langlois, *Textes relatifs à l'Histoire du Parlement*, No.
IV.). A decree by Louis VI. (1112) is signed by twelve (*Ibid.*, No. VI). In
1136 only the chancellor and the four great officers attest (*Ibid.*, No. VIII.). *Cf.*
Luchaire, *Inst. Mon.*, I. 169, note.

[2] See Suger, 80, and n. 5; H. F., XV., 342; Luchaire, *Annales*, No. 489
Langlois, *Textes relatifs à l'Histoire du Parlement*, No. VII. The charter to
Notre-Dame de Paris (Tardif, No. 377), in 1119, is a copy, word for word, of a
similar act by Louis le Debonnaire. (Tardif, No. 104) It even enumerates
Carlovingian imposts. For other cases see Luchaire, *Inst. Mon.*, I., 213, and
n. 2; 244. *Revue Hist.*, XXXVII. (1888), Luchaire, *Louis le Gros et son
Palatins*, p. 267.

[3] Mabillon, 204.

[4] *Ibid.*, 426.

[5] *Revue Hist.*, XLII. (1890), p. 84. Langlois, *Les Origines du Parlement de
Paris.*

[6] Luchaire, *Manuel*, 534. On the palatins, see Luchaire, *Inst. Mon.*, I.,
199-204; Brussel, I., 370-6.

[7] Les noms qui se trouvent au pied de la plupart des arrêts rendus par la
cour capétienne —noms des personages qui ont conseillé au roi sa decision,

Louis conceived the idea of using these trustworthy men as special representatives of the royal person in judicial proceedings. The abuse of power by the local prévôts was very great,[1] and he thought to remedy the evils of administration by making these occasional missions a prominent feature of his government. President Henault[2] has claimed that Louis VI. actually revived the *missi dominici*. But these officers had not the extensive jurisdiction of the Carlovingian *missi;* rather they were royal prévôts endowed with special powers;[3] but they were never in his time a distinct order of the administration. Louis VI. did not revive

après avoir entendu la cause, prouvent que quelques palatins se sont fait de bonne heure une spécialité des affaires judiciaires. Langlois, *Revue Hist.,* XLII., 1890, p. 79. *Les Origines du Parlement de Paris. Cf.* Glasson, V., 402.

[1] Brussel, I., 394.

[2] Henault, I., 196; also Gaillard, I., 186.

[3] Mais à la fin du douzième siècle, quand l'autorité royale, d'abord faible et sans action, eut pris un essor remarquable, sous Louis VI. et sous son fils, par les soins de Suger, quand dominant les tyrannes locales et parvenant à se faire la protectrice des faibles, à modérer les querelles des seigneurs puissants, elle fut devenue, comme l'a dit M. Guizot, "une sorte de justice de paix universelle," elle sentit que pour s'exercer utilement elle devait avoir pour représentants des agents plus considérables que les prévôts. Vuitry, I., 157. *Cf.* Brussel, I., 507–8. Such a case is cited by Mabillon, 600, Charter, No. 180 (1135). *Notitia judicati pro monasterio majori sancti Crispini Suessionensi de feodo Bistisiaci*: Ego Teulfus, abbas . . . . notum fieri volo . . . . quod quidam vir Suessionesis, Aloldus nomine, habebat quosdam reditus apud villam, quae dicitur Bistisisacus, scilicet vinatica, hospites, terragia quae se dicebat in feodo tenere ab ipsa ecclesia. Cumque ab antiqui monachis ecclesiaeque familis diligenter requississem quid super hoc sentirent; jurejurando mihi retulerunt, illum non vera proferre; quin potius per subreptionem non ex recto et jure, ab ecclesia extorsisse. Hic ergo veridica relatione compertis, Aloldum in praesentiam nostri quam saepius arcessiri volui; quem minis blanditiisque pulsabam, ut haec omnia quae ab ecclesia injuste et per violentiam abstulerat, Sanctis restitueret, ne excommunicationi subjaceret. Quod cum nec plene refutans, nec omnino assentiens, in dies agere differret, ita me suspensum reddebat . . . . Indixi itaque illi diem placiti in curia nostra; protestans me facere quid unde judicaret lex causidica vel ecclesiastica. Venit ergo ad praefixum diem, fretus amicorum et jurisperitorum maxima caterva. Quod ego praenoscens, missa ad gloriosissimum Francorum regem Ludovicum epistola, exordine patefeci omnia. Qui *ex lateri suo* Hugonem, agnomento Acharin, *praepositum regium* misit, imperans, ut causam ecclesiae defineret justo judicio.

the ancient Carlovingian order; the humbler work was his to break the way for the greater and permanent institution of the reign of Philip Augustus, that of the grand bailiffs.[1]

An attempt by Louis VI. to modify the judicial duel was measurably successful. He could not hope to abolish it, for the feature was too organic a portion of existing law.[2] Even St. Louis was able to enforce a decree against trial by battle in the area of his immediate realm only.[3] However, from the reign of Louis le Gros the prevalence of duelling begins to decline, and written evidence has increasing weight.[4] If he could not level down, Louis VI. could level up — he could open the lists to those hitherto debarred. In 1108 he granted the serfs of Notre-Dame de Paris the privilege of battle with freemen

[1] On the bailiffs of Philip Augustus, see Brussel, I., 495–505; Walker, 129–137. Langlois, *Revue Hist.*, XLII. (1890), p. 101, *Les Origines du Parlement de Paris*, compares them to the justices in eyre (*justicarii itinerantes*) of Angevin England. But Stubbs holds that "there is no occasion to look for a precedent for the institution of itinerant justices (in England) in the *missi dominici* of Charles the Great or the measures of Louis the Fat."—*Chron. Benedict, Peterburgensis*, Rolls Series, II., Introd. lvii. It would be profitless to inquire into the origin of this institution of Louis VI. even admitting it were ever a customary form, and not an extraordinary usage in his time. Whether the plan were suggested by the ancient Carlovingian practice, or by the innovations of Henry I. of England (see Stubbs, *Select Charters*, 7th ed., p. 141); whether the reforms of Henry I. were prior to those of Louis VI. or not; whether those of either king were suggested by Carlovingian practice or Norman influence — these must be matters largely of speculation. Brunner (*Schwurgericht*, pp. 112 ff.) argues for the priority of the itinerant justices of Normandy to those of England. But this sheds no light on priority between Louis VI. and Henry I. Stubb's remark seems to me to be eminently wise: "In this point, as well as in others, it seems far more natural to suppose that similar circumstances suggested similar institutions." — *Const. History of England*, I. 418.

[2] H. F., X., 121, note a.; XI., 484, note b.

[3] DuCange, *Duellium.* On the legislation of Philip Augustus against the duel, see Delisle, *Catalogue des Actes de Phillippe Auguste*, Paris, 1856, No. 861 and appendix, p. 522; Ordonnances, XI., 250, 283. Philip IV. abolished it in 1302 throughout the realm (Secretan, 469). The clergy advocated the equalization of witnesses before the law. See the letter of Ivo of Chartres.—H. F., XV., 52. *Cf.* Mabillon, 601.

Luchaire, *Manuel*, 538.

before the courts.[1]   In 1109 the right was extended to serfs of
the abbey of Sainte-Genevieve de Paris.[2]   The next year those of
the bishop of Paris were admitted to testify *in forensibus et civili-
bus causis vel placitis adversus liberos homines,*[3] and in 1111 those
of the priory of Saint-Martin-des-Champs.[4]   In 1128 a notable
case occurred.   Louis had admitted the serfs of the chapter of
Chartres to the privileges of witness and trial by battle; the dis-
affected freemen pleaded the former's servile condition as a dis-
barment, whereupon the king declared any person who refused
to accept the royal decree guilty of treason and an enemy of the
state.[5]   Such acts on the part of the king tended to discourage

[1] Ego Ludovicus, Dei clementia Francorum rex, communi quidem episcoporum ac procerum nostrorum consilio et assensu, regie auctoritatis decreto,
instituo, decerno, ut servi sancte Parisiensis ecclesie illi scilicet qui proprie ad
canonicos pertinent, adversus omnes homines tam liberos quam servos, in omnibus causis, placitis et negotiis, liberam et perfectam habeant testificandi et bellandi licentiam, et nemo unquam, servitutis occasionem eis opponens, in eorum
testimonio ullam dare presumat calumpniam.   Hac autem ratione licentiam
testificandi ea que viderint et audierint eis concedimus, quod, si aliquis liber
homo in eadem causa de falso testimonio illos contradicere et conprobare volue-
rit, aut suam conprobationem duello perficiat, aut, eorum sacramentum sine
ulla alia contradictione recipiens, illorum testimonio adquiescat.   Quodsi aliquis temeraria presumptione illorum testimonium in aliquo refutaverit aut
calumpniaverit, non solum regie auctoritatis et publice institucionis reus existat,
sed querelam negocii sui vel placiti inrecuperabiliter amittat; ita scilicet ut
presumptuosus calumpniator de querela sua, si querat ulterius, non audiatur, et
si aliquid ab eo queratur, alterius querele reus et convictus omnino habeatur.
Aliud etiam statuimus ut predictur calumpniator; nisi de tanta calunpnie culpa
Parisiensis ecclesie satisfecerit, excommunicationis mucrone feriatur et testimonium faciendum interea non admittatur.—Tardif, No. 334.

[2] *Ibid.*, No. 341.

[3] *Ibid.*, No. 345.   The quotation is from a letter of Ivo of Chartres which continues: Dilectus filius noster Ludovicus Francorum rex pro utilitate ecclesiastici
ita consulendum arbitratus est, ut episcoporum ac procerum consilio et assensu
institueret Parisiensis ecclesie famulos in omnibus causis, placitis et negotiis
adversus omnes homines tam liberos quam servos et perfectam testificandi et
bellandi licentiam, ita ut nemo eorum testimonio pro ecclesiasticae servitutis
occasione calumniam inferat.—H. F., XV., 52.

[4] *Ibid.*, No. 346.   *Cf.* No. 371.

[5] Luchaire, *Annales*, No. 408.   There is a capital account of a judicial
duel in Galbert de Bruges, chap. lviii.

the judicial duel, for it humilated a freeman to have to fight a villain, while it correspondingly elevated the servile class in their own esteem and the eye of the law.[1]

The practice of appeal, as instituted by Louis VI.,[2] was an entire interpolation in the feudal law of the land. The greatness of this act has not failed to elicit the admiration of historians. Montesquieu[3] characterized it as "a veritable revolution." Hitherto, the dukes of Normandy and Aquitaine, the counts of Brittany, Flanders, Champagne, and Toulouse had enjoyed the privilege of final decision.[4] This condition was of course, a result of the dissipation of the ancient Carlovingian authority. In the days of Charles the Bald, and after him, when royalty was fast becoming a dignity merely, and not a power, the dukes and counts of the provinces used for their own ends, and against the king, the authority delegated to them. By every possible means they prevented access to the royal court Thus the king's

[1] Cf. Lamprecht, 216-7. The customs of Lorris provided for a fine in case of forfeit, if the duel were once agreed upon : — Si vadia duelli temere dederint homines de communia et praepositi assensu, antequam dentur obsides, concordaverint, et si de legitimis hominibus duellium factum fuerit obsides devicti centum et duodecim solidos persolvent.— Art. 14, *Ordonnances*, XI., 201.

[2] Luchaire, *Inst. Mon.*, I., 300-1. Luchaire, *La Cour du Roi et ses fonctions judiciaires sous le règne de Louis VI.*, pp. 23-4. *Acad. des Inscript.*, XXX., 590. Aubert, *Le Parlement de Paris de Philippe-la-Bel à Charles VII.* (1314-1422), ch. i. C. P. Marie-Haas, *L'Administration de la France*, I., 186 Eminent savants, among them Brussel (I., 163, 178, 227), Henrion, *De l'Autorité judiciaire en France*, Introd., p. 55, and Mably (*Observations sur l'Hist. de France*, livre III., ch. iii) have denied this ; the last holding that such usage was not in effect until the reign of Philip Augustus ; but the fact is well authenticated. The cases of the bishop of Arras (H. F., XV., 342-3 ; Langlois, *Textes Relatifs à l'Histoire du Parlement*, No. VII ; cf. Luchaire, *Inst. Mon.*, I., 300) and of the people of Sainte-Severe, are clear evidence (Suger, ch. xi.). Huguenin (p. 17) holds that Suger is responsible for the reform, but as the work is an unqualified eulogy of the abbot of St. Denis, the statement may not be wholly trusted. The truth is, Louis VI. and Suger were so agreed in policy that it is often difficult to distinguish with whom the real honor lies.

[3] "L'introduction des appels dans les mœurs judiciaires fut une véritable révolution." Quoted by Langlois, Revue Hist., XLII (1890), p. 100. *Les Origines du Parlement de Paris.*

[4] Brussel, I., 234-5 ; Luchaire, *Manuel*, 257.

judicial power became almost nullified save in his direct domain. But to this mediatization there was one exception. In the hierarchical constitution of feudalism, the highest suzerain was the king. Beneath him the lords were judges in their own domains, as the king in his, but only on condition of giving ear to all demands for justice.[1] This obligation was the correlative of his obedience to the king. In case of failure of justice (*defectus justitiæ*) only, did the king have original jurisdiction over rear vassals.[2] But Louis, by instituting the practice of appeal, inaugurated something radically new.[3] True appeal is distinctly antifeudal; it implies deference to a higher jurisdiction, the supremacy of another will.[4] It recognizes the majesty of the king; the superiority of the king's law—the legitimate right of royalty to cover with its shield all the law and all the persons

[1] Pardessus, 27–8.

[2] DuCange, *Defectus justitiæ*. Failure of justice might occur, too, if the attendance at the lord's court were too reduced; or when the court failed to convene. In Brittany, however, in the eleventh and twelfth centuries—for Louis VI. made no attempt to coerce a vassal so far removed—there was no appeal, even in case of denial of justice. (Luchaire, *Manuel*, 257.)

[3] L'idée de l'appel était en principe étrangère à la justice féodale .... Ce fut la transition entre l'ancien appel, qui n'est qu'une déclaration d'incompétence, et l'appel véritable, qui repose sur l'idée que le tribunal supérieur a une connaissance supérieure du droit, en vertu de laquelle on lui accorde le pouvoir de réformer le premier jugement. — Secretan, 475–6.

[4] Dans l'appel, on défère à une juridiction supérieure le jugement rendu par un juge inférieur; la cause, déjà jugée en première instance, l'est de nouveau. L'appel suppose l'existence d'une jugement, dont on demande la réformation. La defaulte de droit suppose que le procès n'a pas été ou n'a pu être jugé; le recours au suzerain, dans ce cas, a pour objet qu'il statue sur ce procès, dont son vassal n'a pas pris connaissance, et c'est dans la vérité des mots, une évocation. Il en résulte une différence essentielle, qui a dû faire admettre sans contestation le recours pour defaulte de droit, même contre les grands vassaux. Ce recours qui, par la nature des choses, ne pouvait être porté que devant le roi, ne subordonnait pas, à proprement parler, la juridiction de ses seigneurs à celle du roi; il n'avait lieu précisément que parce qu'ils refusaient d'user de leur droit de justice; ils étaient les maîtres de le rendre sans objet, en faisant juger la cause dans leur cour, la saine raison ne permettant pas qu'il pût exister des procès, ou des plaideurs, qui ne trouveraient pas de juges. Les lois de la féodalité reprouvaient un tel refus; et celui-là seul pouvait, en définitive, faire justice du refus, à cette même féodalité reconnaissait les droits de suzerain. — Pardessus, 79–80. *Cf.* Secretan, 476.

directly or remotely seeking redress. This institution of appeal does not imply a sort of supreme feudal court, as Mably held would be required[1], but inasmuch as the palatins in the time of Louis VI. were beginning to become an inner council[2] and the Parlement of Paris was originally a portion of the *curia regis* set apart to hear petitions, is it not possible that we have, in this creation of Louis VI., almost the initiatory step in the creation of that body?[3] Although the new method obtained slowly, the competence of the royal court in appeal not becoming greatly effective until the middle of the thirteenth century, when the lineaments of the Parlement grow out of the darkness of its origin, still the honor of this truly royal modification of the feudal law is due to Louis VI.[4]

The next important step in the evolution of the Parlement must have been when the court became a stationary body, permanently seated at Paris. The honor of making such a change, however, cannot be attributed to Louis le Gros.[5] In the

[1] See Pardessus, Livre III., ch. iii.

[2] Luchaire, *Inst. Mon.*, I., 199–200.

[3] *Ibid.*, II., 327.

[4] Langlois, Revue Hist., XLII. (1890), p. 99, *Les Origines du Parlement de Paris*). For the steps in the progress of appeal, see p. 100 and notes. The competence of the court in the thirteenth century is shown in Langlois, *Textes relatifs à l'Histoire du Parlement*, Nos. XXIII, XXX.

[5] "On pourrait croire que cette mesure de rendre la cour du roi sédentaire à Paris est antérieure à l'année 1120, si l'on considérait comme véritables, ou du moins comme non altérés, deux diplômes de Louis VI., du 12 Avril 1120, et du 10 Janvier 1121 (H. F., XVII., 269) en faveur de l'abbaye de Tiron, confirmés par Louis VII. le 29 Mars 1164 (*Ibid.*, 272), dans lesquels il est dit, qu'en vertu de la protection et sauvegarde accordée à cette abbaye, les causes qui l'intéressent seront portées *coram magnis præsidentialibus nostris Parisius, vel alibi, ubi nostra præ-excellens et suprema curia residebit,* et qu'il en sera de même des affaires jugées par la justice de ce monastère entre ses hommes. Mais la fausseté de ces dates est évidente, qu'il n'est pas possible d'en argumenter." — Pardessus, 97–8. *Cf.* Les Olim., t. I., XXXIV.; *Bibliothèque de l'École des Chartes*, third series, t. V., 516, ff. — *Chartes fausses de l'abbaye de Tiron;* Luchaire, *Annales*, appendix VIII. (p. 323).

Luchaire (*Inst. Mon.*, I., 307) has this to say: — "A partir du règne de Louis le Gros, Paris devient de plus en plus le séjour habituel du souverain et par suite le siège ordinaire du gouvernement. Il en résulte qu'en fait, et sans

increased importance given the court owing to the extension of its jurisdiction, one is surprised that he should have still retained the ambulatory[1] character of the court. Perhaps, though, the very activity of Louis VI. made this change undesirable, since he always sought to assume personal direction of the proceedings. As the court was the nascent form of the later Parlement, permanence, whenever acquired, must have hastened the course begun in the establishment of appellate jurisdiction.

It is generally supposed that the institutions of feudalism were fixed and well defined, whereas, in point of fact, the relations of high suzerain, vassal and rear vassal were in constant flux.[2]   From time to time, there are positive changes in feudal

qu'aucune règle ait jamais été établie à cet égàrd, la plus grande partie des procès soumis à la cour du roi sont débattus et terminés à Paris, dans le palais même de la cité.   On peut affirmer, d'après le relevé des localités où la cour du roi a exercé ses fonctions judiciaires, que, sous le règne de Louis VII., pour deux ou trois procès qui sont jugés à Orléans ou à Étampes, quinze sont l'objet d'un arrêt rendu à Paris.   La proportion a dû évidemment s'accroître en faveur de la capitale sous les Capétiens du XIII⁰ siècle.   C'est ainsi que peu à peu, par la force même des choses, on est arrivé à la détermination d'un lieu fixe pour les sessions du Parlement."   See in *Ibid.*, II., app., No. XII, the list of sessions of the court from 1137 to 1180.   With the above of Luchaire, *cf.* Lair, *Des Hautes Cours Politiques en France,* p. 5, and Aubert, *Le Parlement de Paris de Phillippe-le-Bel à Charles VII.* (*1314–1422*), p. 7, who concur.

[1] In the campaign into Auvergne (Suger, 108-10) the court is actually in the field : "Si sic judicaverint regni optimates, fiat" says William of Aquitaine. Suger continues : Super his igitur rex cum optimatibus regni consulens, dictante justicia, fidem, juramentum, obsidum sufficientiam suscipit (p. 110).

As long as the king's court was a movable one, the king carried about with him the original text of the law, in rolls (*rotuli*).   It was in consequence of the seizure of a number of these by Richard Cœur de Lion, 5 July, 1194. that the idea was suggested to Philip Augustus of preserving the text of all the laws as state archives, and of opening authentic registers of decisions in civil and criminal cases.   Pfister, *Le Règne de Robert le Pieux,* p. 207.   The actual account of this event is in Roger de Hoveden, *Regnum Anglicarum Scriptores,* 741 (Rolls Series) and in Guillaume le Breton, H. F., XVII., 72.   *Cf.* also Teulet, *Trésor des Chartes,* I., xxv.

[2] In the twelfth century the count of Champagne, who originally was a homager of the king only, held partly of the archbishop of Rheims, partly of the bishops of Langres, Chalons, Auxerre, Autun, the abbot of St. Denis, the duke of Burgundy, the Emperor—and the king.   Brussel, I., 367.

law. If "lordship and homage . . . were the links in the chain of steel which saved the world from being dissolved into a chaos of jarring elements,[1]" nevertheless the form and nature of the links were changed, if not from year to year, certainly from century to century; new measures were introduced, old ones taken away. One such link seems to have been forged by Louis le Gros—that of liege homage,[2] an institution destined at a later day to embroil France and England in serious conflict, when the memorable struggle between Edward III. and Philip of Valois turned on the question whether the English king was bound to do simple or liege homage for Guyenne.[3]

The prolongation and importance of Louis VI.'s military expeditions must have occasioned this new obligation. By it the vassal was held to personal service, irrespective of the traditional forty days, or of the territory to be entered; hitherto the vassal had not been bound to other personal service and could even send a chevalier in his stead.[4]

[1] Pollock, *Science of Politics.*, 47.

[2] Henault, I., 196. This statement needs the following qualification: The term liege homage occurs in texts of the late part of the eleventh century (Glasson, IV., 298.) DuCange cites three cases, but the terms homage and liege homage are used convertibly, and the documents are so confused as hardly to be entitled to very great consideration (Brussel, I., 109). If the creation of the new relation is not due to Louis le Gros (see Tardif, No. 388: "Stephane, jure perpetuo, et in feodo et ut ligio homini nostro concedimus"), the strict legal definition, as well as insistence upon its fulfilment, seem to be due to him. (See *Nouvelle Revue historique de droit français et étranger,* 1883. Vol. VII., p. 659 — *Homme Lige.*) However, liege homage obtained but very slightly, outside of the royal domain, in the twelfth century. In the time of Philip Augustus, the Count of Champagne did liege homage to the king, but it was at that time an innovation. (Glasson, IV., 292, citing Brussel, I., 116.)

For the distinction between fidelity and homage, which are often confused, see Brussel. I. 19 ff., Luchaire, *Manuel,* 186, and Viollet, *Hist. du Droit français,* 559–563, which gives a good bibliography. A bottom fidelity was a relation far surpassing homage in dignity; it implied a moral bond of loyalty, and high position. Homage carried with it all the engagements of vassalage, but one might be a *fidelis* without being a vassal. All vassals were necessarily *fideles*, but all *fideles* were not vassals.—*Cf.* Flach, I., 245.

[3] Lalanne, *Dict. Hist.*, p. 997.

[4] Quant à l'hommage lige, c'était le plus grave [de] tous et il était

On the other hand, Louis VI. raised the position of king of France far higher than hitherto, by enunciating the doctrine, the king can do homage to none. This doctrine, that the crown owed fealty to no one, naturally followed from his definition of royalty as a power original in type.[1]   He declined to do homage for the Vexin[2], which was a vassal county of St. Denis, on the

surtout relatif au service militaire ; l'hommage lige devait le service militaire en personne et pendant toute la durée de la guerre ; tandis que le vassal ordinaire n'était tenu du service militaire que pendant quarante jours à partir de celui où l'on avait été assemblé ; de sorte qu'au bout de ce temps il pouvait rentrer dans son château.   En outre, il ne devait pas le service personnel, et pouvait envoyer un chevalier à sa place. (Glasson, IV., 296.   *Cf.* Lalanne, *Dict. Hist. ut supra.*)

[1] *Cf.* Suger, 80.

[2] Vilcassini siquidem (quod est inter Isaram et Ettam) nobilem comitatum, quem perhibent immunitates ecclesiæ proprium beati Dionysii feodum, quem etiam rex Francorum, Ludovicus Philippi, accelerans contra imperatorem Romanum insurgentem in regnum Francorum, in pleno capitulo beati Dionysii professus est se ab eo habere et jure signiferi, *si rex non esset*, hominium ei debere. —Œuvres de Suger (*Soc. de l'Hist. de F.*) par Lecoy de la Marche.   Suger, *De rebus in administratione sua gestis* (ch. iv., pp. 161–2).   *Cf. Éclaircissements et observations*, pp. 442–3.   Felibien, *Hist. de l'abbaye de Saint-Denis;* also (Felibien) *Oriflamme*, 154, ff. ; Tardif, No. 391 ; Combes, 133 ; Henault, I., 180 ; *Acad. des Inscrip.*, L., p. 499.   The honor of this truly royal act has been generally attributed to Philip Augustus, as in Walker, 9.   The large territorial acquisition by Philip Augustus gave opportunity for numerous applications of this principle, but the germ of the principle is found in the act recorded above of Louis VI.

In the *Bibliothèque de l'École des Chartes* (XXXIV. p. 244 ff., 1873) M. Viollet publishes *Une grande Chronique latine de Saint-Denis* (*Observations pour servir à l'histoire critique des Œuvres de Suger*).   The account there differs somewhat from that quoted above: — "Dixit se (Louis VI.) more priscorum regum auriflammam velle] sumere ab altari, affirmando quod hujus bajulatio ad comitem Vulcassini de jure spectabat, et quod de eodem comitatu, nisi auctoritas regia obsisteret, ecclesiæ, homagium facere tenebatur" (p. 245).   Candor confesses that a difficulty arises from this passage, as M. Viollet admits : "Les mots *more priscorum regum* pourront induire à penser que ce passage est postérieur à Suger, car le Vexin français ayant été réuni à la couronne sous Philippe Ier, l'usage deporter l'oriflamme était, dira-t-on, tout nouveau pour les rois de France au temps de Louis VI. et de Suger.   Suger aurait-il donc considéré cet usage comme bien antérieur à Phillippe Ier et à Louis VI. (*priscorum regum*) ?   Mais une tradition aussi fausse n'a pu se faire jour que longtemps après Louis VI. ; et d'ailleurs, dans

ground of the superiority of the king to any suzerain, lay or ecclesiastical. The importance of this act of Louis VI. can hardly be estimated too highly. Its significance lies in the fact that it was an assertion of superiority in *kind*, of the king, over all; he was his own peer; none on the soil of France was his suzerain.

le même phrase, le roi considère ce droit comme lui étant échu par l'intermédiare des comtes du Vexin; il y a là une contradiction flagrante qui decèle un rajeunissements postérieur à Suger. Le lecteur reste libre de s'en tenir à cette objection et de mettre ce passage au nombre des rajeunissements que j'ai signalés tout-à-l'heure; mais, pour mon compte, je ne m'arrête pas à cette difficulté et voici ma réponse : La phrase qu'on vient de lire, loin de recéler une erreur, paraît contenir, en abrégé, les points fondamentaux de l'histoire exacte de l'oriflamme. En effet, on se trompe en disant que les rois de France portèrent l'oriflamme depuis annexion du Vexin et non antérieurement. Toutefois, cette annexion a joué un certain rôle dans l'histoire de l'oriflamme, et ce rôle est ici relaté . . . Certes, un pareil exposé est très-vague et incomplet; nous ne tenons guère ici qui les extrémités d'une chaîne dont les anneaux intermédiaires nous échappent; mais c'en est assez pour que nous nous gardions de rejeter comme n'ayant pu être écrite par Suger une phrase qui précisément relate ces deux données fondamentales. Ce passage a pu, d'ailleurs, être retouché quant à la rédaction; on est surpris d'y trouver le nom de Suger; le style direct et première personne seraient plus naturels."

See further on this act (Tardif, No. 379); Suger, 105, note 1, and Lebeuf, *Histoire de Paris*, III., 250 ff.

CHAPTER IV.

ADMINISTRATIVE ORGANIZATION.

CENTRAL ADMINISTRATION.

Of the administrative body of the king, the features of which may be vaguely traced in the beginning of the eleventh century,[1] five members were important: the seneschal, the butler, the constable, the chamberlain, and the chancellor.[2] Of these the seneschal and the chancellor were by far the most influential.[3] Besides administrative and judicial authority, they possessed domains and benefices, sometimes of vast extent.[4]

The seneschal was the director-general of the realm. His prototype was the ancient mayor of the palace. He was the second person in the kingdom,[5] and in case of a weak king, like

---

[1] Luchaire, *Manuel*, 257.

[2] It is difficult to determine the order of precedence of these officers. The chancellor always closes the list, which, as above given, is the order in the reign of Louis le Gros, when their character and position are most defined. (Luchaire, *Inst. Mon.*, I., 164. Langlois, *Textes Relatifs du Parlement de Paris*, No. VIII.) The butler and constable appear in 1043. Four years later are found the seneschal and chamberlain, and all five sign together for the first time in 1060. (Luchaire, *Inst. Mon.*, I., 167.) Their attributes are, at first, somewhat indistinct; in the eleventh century there begins to be a separation of duties, and in the reign of Philip I. the institution tends to regulate itself. But, as pointed out, the documents are obscured by a host of intrusive names. Under Philip I. there appears, for a short time an officer (*dispensator*) who seems to have been not unlike the modern butler.—Luchaire, *Manuel*, 588.

[3] Luchaire, *Manuel*, 522. On the chancellor, see Brussel, I., 535, 628.

[4] Luchaire, *Manuel*, 260; Brussel I., 629.

[5] Simon, seneschal of Philip I., is styled "consul et regis Francorum primipilus."—H. F., XV., 541. The account of Hugh de Cleers (H. F., XII., 493), regarding the institution of the seneschalship and the relations of the Count of Anjou to Louis VI. may be considered apocryphal, although accepted by Sismondi, V., 135 ff; Combes. 77–8; and other early historians. The

Louis VII. he might become the controlling will in the administration. He had control of the machinery of local administration, the supervision of the prevots and other agents of the king; he acted as president of the *curia regis* in case of the absence of the king, and on occasion, took the field as royal commandant.[1]

The power of these officers, especially the seneschal, united with the evil of the hereditability of fiefs,[2] in the twelfth century became a serious menace to the crown.[3] In order to reduce the danger, the kings had recourse either to violent deprivation of title, or the policy, more and more frequently adopted, of leaving an office vacant for a number of years, or of dividing its duties, thus leaving the holder nothing but the ascription of authority.[4]

Of the three lesser officers their titles sufficiently describe the nature of their duties. The chamberlain seems to have sunk the most rapidly in dignity and power. Under Henry I. he commands the army; at the end of the eleventh century the seneschal has supplanted him, although he is still an influential personage; under Louis VI. he has slipped down to third place.[5]

The constable was a survival of the old marshal, and is first mentioned in the time of Henry I. (1043). He was then, as the name implies, master of the horse.[6] Later certain minor judicial

writer attempts to prove the office at the time of Louis VI. an hereditary fief in the house of Anjou, who held the place, as it were, *ex officio,* and that the actual incumbent did him (the Count of Anjou) homage. The account is singularly full of details, and describes the interview of Louis VI. with Foulque, and the subsequent homage of Garland, in 1118. But the purported facts are sustained by no charter. The probability is that the concessions pretended to have been made by Louis VI. were fabricated between 1150 and 1168 in the interests of Henry II. of England and Count of Anjou, the rival of Louis VII. See Luchaire, *Annales,* 325–6: *Inst. Mon.,* I., x, n. 2 and p. 180.

[1] Luchaire, *Inst. Mon.,* I., 177–184.

[2] Brussel (I., 71). thinks that benefices were hereditary in the time of Hugh Capet, and cites the famous letter of. Eudes II., count of Chartres to Robert II. According to Luchaire (*Inst. Mon.,* II., 4 ff.) the kings struggled against the inheritance of fiefs until the second half of the eleventh century.

[3] Luchaire, *Manuel,* 260.

[4] *Ibid.* 519.

[5] Luchaire, *Manuel,* 523. He is called "princeps exercitus Francorum."— Luchaire, *Inst. Mon.,* I., 169, citing H. F. XI., 207.

[6] Luchaire, *Inst. Mon.,* I., 171.

powers were given him, which were increased as the seneschal was deprived of his power.   Finally he succeeded to the military rights of the seneschal, and in the fourteenth century was chief of the royal forces.[1]

The butler never seems to have enjoyed the measure of power that the seneschal and chancellor had.   In early Capetian times his name was most often after that of the seneschal; but in the time of Philip I. he signs next to the last.[2]   The place never seems to have been a menace, for even after the revolution in the palace, under Louis VII. and Philip Augustus, it was attached to the family of La Tour, of Senlis.[3]

The crisis in what was the immediate household of the king, fell in the reign of Louis le Gros, and was brought about by the inordinate ambition of Stephen de Garland.   History affords few cases of so complete a political ascendency acquired by the members of a single family as that attained by the brothers Garland during the reign of Louis VI.   The exigencies of circumstance and the rare abilities of the four brothers, Anselm, William, Stephen and Gilbert, alike account for the fact.   When Louis VI. began to reign he was assailed by enemies both open and secret; even his own kindred plotted against him.[4]   To this was added the hatred of the house of Rochefort, the turbulence of the seigneur of Puiset and of many another baron, the traditional enmity of the Anglo-Norman king, and the hostility of the counts of Anjou and Blois.   In the midst of such trials, the intelligence and ability of the Garlands stood Louis in good stead.[5]   Anselm was a faithful seneschal until the day when he fell in the service of his master in the third siege of the chateau de Puiset.[6]   William succeeded him, and was present at the memorable defeat of Brenneville,[7] August 20, 1119.   Stephen, meanwhile, was chan-

---

[1] Luchaire, *Manuel*, 526.   [2] *Ibid.*, 525.

[3] Luchaire, *Inst. Mon.*, I., 177   On these lesser officers, see Brussel, I., 628–635.

[4] Ord. Vit. IV., 196 ff.   Suger, c. xvii.

[5] Suger, 21, 36.   [6] *Ibid.*, 79.

[7] Luchaire, *Remarques sur la succession des Grands Officiers de la Couronne* (1108–1180), p. 1.

cellor, an office which became his ecclesiastical pretensions, for the chancellorship was never held by a layman. It was he who, before Suger became a prominent figure in the government, first moulded the policy of the king in his conflict with the denationalizing reform party in the church.[1]

In 1120 William de Garland died. Then an extraordinary arrangement of the royal household was made. In order to fill the vacant seneschalship, Louis VI. advanced his chancellor,[2] allowing him, at the same time, to retain the more clerkly position. A change so unique elicited astonishment even in that age of men-at-arms,—a churchman in the first military rank of the realm![3] This double investiture, continuing for seven years, fattened the ambition of the churchman. As chancellor and chief chaplain he enjoyed the livings of a vast number of ecclesiastical benefices, dependent immediately upon the crown. He was archdeacon of Paris,[4] archdeacon of Notre-Dame de Paris,[5] deacon of Saint-Samson d'Orléans,[6] deacon of the abbey of Sainte-Genevieve,[7] deacon of the chapter of Sainte-Croix d'Orléans,[8] and deacon of Saint-Aignan d'Orléans.[9] In order that he might be able to carry the church of Orleans in his pocket, as it were, he

[1] Luchaire, *Louis le Gros et son Palatins*, Revue Hist., XXXVII., 1888.

[2] Luchaire, *Remarques sur la succession des Grands Officiers de la Couronne* (1108–1180), p. 11.

[3] " Quis sane non miretur imo et detestetur unius esse personae et armatum ducere militiam et alba stolaque indutum, in medio ecclesiae pronunciare evangelium ? Magis honorabile ducit putari se militem, curiam ecclesiae praefert."— St. Bernard, Epistle 78. H. F., XV., 547. *Cf. Chron. Maurin*, H. F., XII., 76–7 :

Interea defuncto Willelmo Anselli Dapiferi germano, Stephanus Cancellarius. . . . major regiae domûs effectus. Hoc retroactis generationabus fuerat inauditum, ut homo, qui Diaconatus fungebatur officio, militiae simul post regem duceret principatum. Hic vir industrius et saecularii praeditus sapientia, cum multis ecclesiasticorum honorum redditibus, tum familiaritate regis, quam sic habebat, ut ei potius a quibusdam, diceretur imperare quam servire, temporali felicitate supra cæteros mortates nostris temporibus efflorebat.

[4] Luchaire, *Annales*, Nos. 53, 206.

[5] *Ibid.*, Nos. 272, 284.

[6] *Ibid.*, No. 62.

[7] *Ibid.*, Nos. 94, 109.

[8] *Ibid.*, Nos. 125, 173.

[9] *Ibid.*, No. 176.

had prevailed upon the king to advance Hugh of Orleans to the bishopric of Laon and confer the deaconate of the cathedral church upon himself.[1]   But he aspired to a bishopric.   In 1100 he had made an unsuccessful attempt to secure that of Beauvais.[2] In 1114, when Geoffroi, its bishop, died, he demanded the place. But pope Pascal II., who was no lover of the priestly politician because of his hostility to the Clugny reform movement, as well as on account of his unbounded craving for power, was scandalized at the chancellor's request.   The action of the pontiff elicited from Stephen the haughty rejoinder that he did not serve the king so much as govern him.[3]

At last the ambition of the seneschal overreached itself.   Like his predecessors and colleagues in the royal household, he sought to retain the seneschalship in the Garland family.   As an ecclesiastic, he could not transmit the office directly ; but in 1127 he gave his niece in marriage to Amauri de Montfort, together with the chateau de Rochefort and the assurance that her husband should succeed him.[4]   The king evidently was not cognizant of the plan.   It was a crisis in the history of the monarchy.   Would the king allow a place of so much power to be disposed of without his consent?   Would he suffer himself to be dictated to?   Would he dare allow the ·vicious principle of hereditability of fiefs to become attached to the highest dignity of the realm?   The attempt of the seneschal was a grave blunder.   Louis le Gros' sluggish suspicions were at last aroused.   Stephen was deprived of his honors and driven from the court[5] with his brother Gilbert, the butler.[6]   Stung by the disgrace, Stephen and his accomplice made common cause with Henry I. of England and Thibaud IV., the Count of Blois.[7]   The strain on the monarchy was intense.   The king had besides to face the now open hostility of the reform clergy.   Paris lay under an interdict.[8]   Henry I.

[1] Luchaire, *Annales*, No. 133.   [2] *Ibid.*, No. 17.
[3] *Chron. Maurin*, H. F., XII., 73.
[4] Suger, 116.   *Chron. Maurin*, H. F. XII., 77.
[5] Suger, 116.
[6] Luchaire, *Remarques sur la Succession des Grands Officiers de la Couronne,*
[7] Suger, 117.   *Chron. Maurin*, H. F., XII., 77.
[8] Luchaire, *Annales*, No. 439.

hovered on the French border.[1] The surrounding country was pillaged by the outlawed Garlands.[2] Ralph, the count of Vermandois, cousin and staunch ally of Louis, had fallen in the siege of the chateau de Livri, the seat of the house of Garland.[3] If ever Louis VI. merited the title of "Wide-awake" (*l'Éveille*)[4] it was then. Honorius II. was coaxed into rescinding the interdict, to the deep chagrin of St. Bernard and the reformers.[5] Profiting by a moment of calm, Louis took care to have his son Philip associated with him in the government,[6] that the question of succession might be assured. Then he turned his arms against the rebels. After a desultory conflict of four years, Stephen succumbed to the untiring energy of the king, (1132)[7] and was restored to the chancellor's desk. His political rôle was ended; his influence and power had passed to abler and safer hands, and at his death the seal of his office passed quietly over to Algrin, the vice-chancellor.[8]

This revolt in the palace, which culminated in the fall of the Garlands, marks a decisive point in the history of the monarchy. The continuity of office was broken. In this respect Louis le Gros founded the traditions which were followed out by his successors.[9]

[1] Luchaire, *Annales*, No. 414.   [2] *Ibid.*, No. 428.
[3] *Ibid.*, No. 420. Suger, 117.

[4] Louis is called by turns "*le Gros*" (*pinguis, crassus*), which is most common; "the Fighter" (*le Batailleur*); "the Great" (*le Grand*); "the White" (*le Blanc*), alluding to his pale complexion, due to poisoning in youth (Ord. Vit. IV., 197); and he is also called "*le Justicier*."

[5] See the letter of St. Bernard, H. F., XV., 545, 550.

[6] Luchaire, *Annales*, No. 433. Philip Augustus was the first monarch of France who did not have his successor crowned in his lifetime.—Brussel, I., 66.

[7] Luchaire, *Annales*, No. 487. The principal episode of this war was the capture of Livri; see *Bibliothèque de l'École des Chartes*, XXXVIII., 480.

[8] Luchaire, *Remarques sur la Succession des Grand Officiers de la Couronne*, p. 34.

[9] "The consideration of the great offices of the crown under Philip Augustus has shown the completion under him of a process already begun by his grandfather and father. The great court offices, which the limited extent of the royal possessions under the early Capetians and the intimate association of the nobles of the Ile de France with the king in the administration of the government made useful under Henry I. or Philip I., had proved dangerous to the

After the fall of the Garlands for four years the seneschal's place was vacant,[1] and then another faithful count of Vermandois was appointed.[2] But the preponderant influence in the realm now rested with Suger.[3]

Suger's position was unique.[4] Up to this time, warlike character, wealth, and achievement had been the qualifications for the office of chief minister. Suger was of humble birth,[5] slight of stature, and in health was not strong; but he had a luminous intellect, and a will which prompted him to act with judgment and despatch. The first relations of Louis and the future

growing strength of the monarchy and unwieldy in administrative practice. Louis VI. and Louis VII. had tried to limit their power. Philip Augustus practically abolished the two posts of greatest prominence, and, by his employment of men of lower position, made the three remaining offices chiefly honorary. No feature of this policy was original with Philip. It was that of his grandfather and father.—Walker, 55. On the position of the seneschal after Philip Augustus, see Pardessus, 268-270.

Stubbs, *Const. Hist. of England*, Vol. I., chap. xi. pp. 380-1, makes an instructive comparative study of contemporary English and French institutions : "In England . . . . where the amount of public business was increasing rapidly in consequence of the political changes, and where it was of the utmost importance to avoid the creation of hereditary jurisdictions, it was absolutely necessary that a new system should be devised. The same need was felt in France ; and the same tide of events which threw the administration here into the hands of Bishop Roger, brought the management of affairs there into the hands of the Abbot Suger. In each case we see an ecclesiastical mayor of the palace; a representative of the king in all capacities : lieutenant in his absence, chief agent in his presence ; a prime minister in legal, financial, and even military affairs, but prevented by his spiritual profession from founding a family of nobles, or withdrawing from the crown the powers which he had been commissioned to sustain."

[1] The writs read *vices dapiferi possidens.*—Luchaire, *Manuel*, 521.

[2] Luchaire, *Inst. Mon.*, I., 185.   [3] *Ibid.*

[4] Suger's eminent position is expressed in many ways by his biographer : " Præerat palatio ; " " nec illum a claustri cura prohiberat curia, nec a consiliis principum hunc excusaret monasterium ; " " cumque ab eo jura dictarentur nullo unquam pretio declinavit a recto ; " " præcipua regni incumberent negotia ; " " ex eo siquidem tempore, quo primum regiis est adhibitus consiliis, usque advitæ illius terminum constat regnum semper floruisse et in melius atque amplius, dilatatis terminis et hostibus subjugatis, fuisse provectum. Quo sublato de medio statim sceptrum regni gravem ex illius absentia sensit jacturam." Willelmus—*Vita Sugerii*, Liber I., *passim.*

[5] Suger, Introd., p. 1.

minister date from their school days in the fine old Capetian abbey of St. Denis.[1]   When Suger was appointed minister he had served a long apprenticeship.   He had been episcopal prevot of Berneval-by-the-sea,[2] in Normandy, and later of Touri,[3] on the grand route from Chartres to Orleans.   Here Suger was forced to assume the rôle of a warrior.   Touri was fast being reduced to a waste by the depredations of the lord of Puiset, whose castle was hard by.[4]   Here also began Suger's public career.   In 1118 he was sent on a diplomatic mission to Pope Gelasius II., then at Maguelonne.[5]   Twice[6] he was sent to Rome itself.   When Henry V. the emperor died, all western Europe awaited with anxiety the new election.   Frederick of Swabia, Conrad of Franconia and Lothar, Count of Suplinberg, were candidates.[7]   For France the issue of the election was important. Henry had been hostile to France.   Would the new emperor continue his policy?   Frederick was his nephew.   The peace of France therefore required that Frederick be defeated.   Suger believed that the juncture demanded his presence at Maintz, and

[1] Suger, Introd., p. 1.

[2] Huguenin, 10. Huguenin thinks it is not unlikely that Suger's knowledge of law and diplomacy was here acquired. "Le religieux se trouve ainsi en communication avec le peuple le plus renommé, au moyen-age, pour la science juridique, et il a lui-même un tribunal où il prononce des jugements. Initié à la coutume de Normandie et aux lois de Guillaume le Conquérant, il ne peut se trouver sans doute à une meilleure école, pour se perfectionner dans la science du droit, pour saisir les finesses et attendre à toutes les profondeurs de la jurisprudence . . . . Le légiste se montre déjà bien visiblement dans Suger,"—pp. 10–11.

[3] *Ibid.*, 22.

[4] Tauriacus igitur famosa Beati Dionysii villa, caput quidem aliarum; et propria et specialis sedes Beati Dionysii, peregrinis et mercatoribus seu quibuscumque viatoribus alimenta cibariorum in media strata, lassis etiam quietem quiete ministrans, intolerabilibus dominorum præfati castri Puteoli angariis usque adeo miserabiliter premebatur ut . . . . jam colonis pene destituta langueret . . . . annonam et talliam sibi primum, deinde dapifero suo, deinde præposito suo, rusticorum vectigalibus ad castrum deferri cogeret."—Suger, *De rebus in administratione*, c, xii.

[5] Suger, 93.

[6] *Ibid.*, 69, 99–100.

[7] *Hist. du Roi Louis VII.*, c. 2. Huguenin, 68.

although he had no official voice in the diet, he contrived to win
the favor of the grand chancellor of the empire, the archbishop
Adalbert, who directed the election.[1] Adalbert threw his influence
in favor of Lothar of Saxony, and the hostility between the
two great sections of the empire of Charles the Great was laid for
a season. The great abbot's international influence also extended
to England. Henry I. honored him with his confidence, and
sought his advice.[2] And yet, from a legal point of view, while
Louis VI. reigned, Suger was never more than the abbot of St.
Denis. He bore no secular title, even when the direction of the
state was in his hands.[3] He was neither seneschal nor chancellor.[4]

In 1132 Ralph of Vermandois replaced Stephen de Garland
as seneschal. He added strength to the office without danger to
the monarchy. He was, by the situation of his fief, the traditional foe of the houses of Champagne and Coucy.[5] It was
through his solicitation, backed by substantial help, that Louis
VI. undertook (1128) the campaign which at last reduced Thomas
de Marle.[6] In 1132, by an alliance which nothing but political
considerations could have prompted, Enguerran, the heir of the
house of Coucy, married the niece of the seneschal, and the interests of the Capetian monarchy became the interests of that historic family,[7] whose once proud motto was—

> "Je ne suis roy ne comte aussy,
> Je suis le Sire de Coucy."

[1] Huguenin, 69. "Ego Maynardus cum Suggerio . . . . in præsentia D.
Alberti venerabilis Maguntini archiepiscopi, in illo celebri colloquio quod de
electione Imperatoris apud Maguntiam habitum est, hanc pacis compositionem
feci." etc.—*Cartul. de Saint Denis*, t. II., p. 475. See the account given in
Hist. du Roi Louis VII., c. 2, and notes.

[2] "Familiarem me habebat (Henricus), venienti etiam . . . . occurebat, et
quod multos suorum celeret de reformatione pacis, sæpius mihi aperiebat. Unde
crebro, Deo auxiliante, contigit nostro labore de multis guerris et implicatis
multorum almulorum machinamentis ad bonam pacis compositionem pervenire.
(*Sugerii epist. ad Gaudef. comit. Andegav.*, H. F., XV., 521).

[3] H. F., XII., 112.

[4] Luchaire, *Inst. Mon.*, I., 185, 192-3,.

[5] Luchaire, *Louis le Gros et son Palatins, Revue Hist.*, xxxvii, (1890) p. 269.

[6] Suger, 114-6.

[7] *Continuator, Præmonstr.*, H. F., xiii, 329. Enguerran was present at the

LOCAL ADMINISTRATION.

With the development of the central administration there had been a corresponding — even earlier — evolution of local administrative forms. These local officers were the prevots and their subordinates, vicars, beadles, and the mayors and sergeants of towns,[1] collectively known as *ministerii* or *servientes*.[2]

The origin of the prevots is difficult to trace; but they can be found as far back as the time of Henry I. (1046)[3] The institution may have been suggested by the episcopal government, which from remote times was wont to designate by that title the managers of the estates of the church.[4] Like other officers, the prevot held his place in fief. He was named and could be deposed by his sovereign, although theory and fact, at the end of the eleventh century, were often at variance, and the post not infrequently was hereditary.[5] The judicial power of the prevot extended from simple misdemeanors up to graver crimes; but his most important function was to collect the revenue.[6] Owing to the rudimentary condition of local governmental forms, the early kings had been induced to farm the revenues.[7] This complication is the key to the apparently incongruous relations of king and prevots, which are presented throughout the twelfth century. Their semi-feudal tenure, and the petty tyrannies they employed in exacting tribute were inimical to the interests of the crown. Their excesses attained such proportions that sometimes whole districts were abandoned by the inhabitants.[8] This accounts for the exemptions lavished by the kings upon abbeys and communes.[9] Louis granted a large number of such privileges.[10] It was also in order to prevent abuses from this source that he

assembly of Vezelai, when Louis VII. took the cross. *Hist. du Roi Louis VII.*, chap. x, p. 159.

[1] Luchaire, *Inst. Mon.*, I., 217-8.
[2] Walker, 126, note 3.
[3] Luchaire, *Inst. Mon.*, I., 209.
[4] Luchaire, *Manuel*, 539.
[9] Luchaire, *Inst. Mon.*, I., 231-2.
[5] Luchaire, *Inst. Mon.*, I., 237.
[6] Luchaire, *Inst. Mon.*, I., 225.
[7] Luchaire, *Inst. Mon.*, I., 225.
[8] Brussel, I., 394.

[10] Luchaire, *Annales*, Nos. 42, 90, 102, 118, 123, 129, 139, 165, 176, 181, 182, 198, 201, 202, 211, 227, 241, 273, 355, 365, 419, 451, 572, 606.

planned the protecting intervention of special lieutenants,[1] an institution which Philip Augustus, thanks to the preparatory work of his grandfather, was able to make efficient, for the value of the prevot depended upon his proximity to the king. " Their aggressiveness and persistence in attacking the powers of the clergy and small nobles, as well as their exactions from the non-noble class, doubtless aided the process of consolidation of the royal power in the crown domain."[2]

[1] See this dissertation, pp. 35–7.

[2] Walker, 127. On the prevots, see Luchaire, *Inst. Mon.*, I., 214–7 ; 225–41. Walker, 126–8. The excellent discussion of Luchaire precludes any extended treatment in the present work. Besides the prevots and their underlings, bishops and abbots were considered agents of the king. " Ce phénomène historique est aussi curieux qu'incontestable." (Luchaire, *Inst. Mon.*, I., 209). They used their power to excommunicate in the interests of the civil authority. —*Cf.* H. F., XV., 152.

CHAPTER V.

FEUDAL AND PUBLIC ECONOMY.

A monarch of Louis VI.'s stamp could not be content with the unsatisfactory work of granting exemptions or breaking down the hereditary prevotal caste merely.[1] He had genuinely constructive ideas. A general economic survey of the kingdom was projected in the last years of his life, but never completed, owing to his failing strength. The scheme included a registration of all the lands throughout the realm, and a rearrangement of the taxes upon a basis less feudal, we may believe, in its nature.[2] In the spring of 1137, when Louis the Young was making ready for his pilgrimage into Aquitaine, a royal decree provided for a general tax.[3] Such an act was more than feudal in character.[4]

[1] See the letter of Louis VI. to Eudes, chatelain of Beauvais.—*Ordonn.*, XI., 177.

[2] Il (Louis le Gros) tente la grande opération du cadastre de tout le territoire appartenant à la couronne. Des arpenteurs et des mesureurs de terres sont commissionnés pour relever les contenances des différents fiefs, afin d'appliquer à chacun, suivant son revenu, une équitable répartition du cens. On voit comment déjà apparaissent ces premières lueurs d'administration financière, qui, bientôt, de la commune vont passer à l'État. M. le Baron de Nervo.—*Les Finances françaises sous l'ancienne Monarchie, la République, le Consulat et l'Empire.* 3 vols. Paris, 1863, Vol. I., p. 8.

[3] Igitur imminente destinatae sibi virginis ductione, pater Ludovicus itineri necessaria praeparat, ut et tanta res cito effectui mancipetur, elaborat. Imperialis itaque edicti taxatione ubique publicata, militum agmina non parva properanter conveniunt, et ad ampliationem regii comitatus, urbes et oppida suorum multitudinem habitatorum emittunt.—*Ex Chronico Mauriniacensi*, H. F., XII., 83.

[4] The general tax imposed by Louis VII. at Suger's suggestion (H. F., XII., 295) is commonly regarded as the first fiscal levy in 223 years not of a feudal nature (Clamageran, I., 193), although Vuitry (I., 390) holds that that also was a sort of feudal aid.—Consult Luchaire, *Inst. Mon.*, I., 126-7, and notes. See note 3, p. 58.

Was this act inspired by the Domesday Survey of William the Conqueror ? There is nothing to indicate it ; but the idea is suggestive. Suger's early connection with ecclesiastical administration in Normandy, and his intimacy with Henry I., to my mind, account for this glimmer of a new régime, and we know that the Domesday Survey owed its principle to a Norman source.[1]

Such a scheme as Louis VI. projected, if he had lived to carry it into effect, would certainly have exalted the monarchy by diminishing the independence of the separate feudal governments, much the same as the danegeld in England, by its uniformity and the extent of its application, contributed to political unity.[2] As it was, its importance cannot escape attention. It was a genuinely creative piece of statesmanship, for the last tax, approaching a general tax in character, in France, up to the time of Louis VI. had been in 924—the tribute paid to the Northmen.[3] It was, therefore, the first fiscal project in over two centuries not of a feudal character. In the succeeding interval the right of the feudal lord had been established and extended. In the eleventh century there was a time when little distinction was made between the revenues of the crown and the king's private purse.[4] Taxation as a public

[1] Stubbs, *Const. Hist. of England*, I., 298.

[2] *Cf.* Green, *Making of England*, 414 ; Clamageran, I., 193.

[3] Vuitry, I., 479. The usual statement is that the tax of 924 was the last general tax levied in *France*, the inference being that it applied to the entire realm of Charles the Simple. As a matter of fact, the tax was laid upon *Francia*, because of the revolt of Robert, son of Robert le Fort and brother of Odo of Paris, and was not general at all. See Marion, *De Normanorum Ducum cum Capetianis pacto ruptaque societate*, Paris, 1892, p. 8 ; and Lippert, *Geschichte des Westfrankischen Reiches unter Konig Rudolf*, Leipzig, 1885, p. 38. This confusion of *France*, in the *wider significance*, and *Francia* has arisen, I think, from the careless use of the Guizot translation of Frodoard, which is misleading, instead of the original Latin version. Francia is there translated "France," and a careless reading of the statement there made might lead a writer, as it has Clamageran (I. 193), and Vuitry (I. 479), into error. On the use of the term *Francia*, see Freeman's *Norman Conquest* I., appendix I., especially p. 684.

[4] I question whether "Le roi vivait des ses revenus comme un simple seigneur."—Boutaric, *Hist. de Saint Louis et l'Alfonse de Poitiers*. Quoted in Montchretien, introd. li., note 2.

measure disappeared, or rather, was converted into the number-
less feudal exactions of the Middle Ages.[1] But the French
monarchy was something more than the "great fief" of Mezeray.
The *droit de régale* was a prerogative approaching monarchial
authority[2] and not circumscribed by the limits of the Ile de
France. "The church throughout the most of northern and
central France was the direct tenant of the crown in temporal
matters. On the vacancy of a bishopric or of a royal abbey, the
king, as the rightful overlord assumed full administration of such
rights and possessions of the see as were not distinctively ecclesiastical. . . . This right was an effective means of filling the royal
treasury, and even more advantageous to the monarchy as afford-
ing political power. The return every few years of the *temporalia*
of these great sees to the royal control, enabled the king to resist
the encroachments of the neighboring vassals on the ecclesiastical
fiefs; and for a time at least, to use the whole force of a bishopric, in addition to his own proper resources, against any lay subject whom he might wish to curb."[3] Louis le Gros was a careful
guardian of the crown's regalian privileges,[4] for political and
financial reasons alike, although in the cautious working out of
his policy of intensive development he made little effort to extend
the right. In Normandy, Anjou and Maine the right fell to the
crown with the forfeiture of those fiefs by King John; while in
Aquitaine and Brittany the right was enjoyed by the dukes in
their fiefs. But in the ecclesiastical provinces of Sens and
Rheims, in Burgundy, Champagne, Nevers, Auxerre, Tonnerre

[1] Les impôts publics étaient presque entièrement tombés en désuétude, et
les ressources du trésor étaient réduites aux revenus des domaines royaute, aux
dons gratuits et à des services réels et personnels."—Tardif, I., VIII., *Notice
préliminaire. Cf.* H. F., XIV., Introd. xxxvii.

[2] This is a mooted point, however. M. Langlois (*Le Règne de Phillippe III. le
Hardi*) contests the attitude of M. Luchaire, *Inst. Mon.*, I., 124-8. But the
admirable discussion of M. Pfister, *Le Règne de Robert le Pieux*, Paris, 1885,
Livre II., chap. v., in my opinion, fully vindicates the royal character of the
régale. On the origin of the *régale* consult Phillips, *Der Ursprung des Rega-
lenrechts in Frankreich*, Halle, 1870.

[3] Walker, pp. 97-99.

[4] Luchaire, *Inst. Mon.*, II., 263.

and Auvergne the *droit de regale* was a valuable source of fiscal and political power to the crown.[1]

Owing to the alienations and donations of Louis' predecessors, the royal receipts had became seriously impaired,[2] so that the kings, weak as they were, were sometimes constrained to exercise the hazardous right of confiscation.[3] Although Louis VI. did not scruple to wrest money from the Jews,[4] he sought to secure a more dignified income than festival gifts,[5] and market dues.[6] The *ordonnances* of his reign show how solicitous he was to promote commerce and foster agriculture.[7] A large number of charters of exemptions, and grants of privilege attest his interest in public economy.[8] Undoubtedly Suger was the inspiring cause of such measures. No part of the policy of Louis VI. is less his own than that pertaining to finance. He simply applied *in extenso* what his minister had already adopted in the estates of St. Denis.[9] These were organized by Suger under a régime calculated to produce the best results. In all the domains of the abbey, the prevots and their subordinates were obliged to transmit exact accounts of the condition of affairs.[10] Suger thus had

---

[1] Luchaire, *Inst. Mon.*, I., 124-5.

[2] Tardif, I., viii. H. F., XI., Intr. cxli.

[3] Vuitry I., 314. Louis VI. and Louis VII. did exercise the right of confiscation, but always with reference to the small vassals of the royal domain The confiscation of Normandy by Philip Augustus was really a landmark in feudal law. See Luchaire, *Inst. Mon.*, II., 22, note 2.

[4] Abelard (*de Calamitatibus*, H. F., XIV., 292) complains "gravioribus exactionibus monachos ipsos quam tributarios Judaeos exagitabat" (Louis VI.). On the king's treatment of the Jews, see Luchaire, *Manuel*, 582-3; Brussel, Bk. II., ch. 39. Philip Augustus enumerated them in the budget (1206), according to Brussel, I., 59. *Cf.* Luchaire, *Manuel*, 583.

[5] H. F., XV., 147.

[6] Clamegeran, I., 206, n.

[7] *Ordonnances*, t. XI., p. 183.

[8] Luchaire, *Annales*, Nos. 58, 162, 167, 196, 244, 271, 273, 277, 321, 516, 551, 557, 574, 586, 587, 601, 607, 608, 611, 612.

[9] Huguenin, 34.

[10] Huguenin, 33. On page 26, note 2, M. Huguenin gives an actual instance — the roll of Mathieu le Beau, of the French Vexin : "Ego Matthaeus Bellus, homo ligius existens S. Dionisii et ejus abbatis, rogatu D. Sugerii abbatis et totius conventus omnes feodos meos quos de S. Dionisio, in propriam possideo,

what really was a budget, the enlarged lines of which afterwards, when he was regent under Louis VII., included the public domain. The interrupted survey of Louis VI. probably had its inception here; but it required two generations for the new measures to commend themselves to the royal treasury.[1]

In addition to such measures, Louis VI. coined a new right for the king—that of *pariages*, or sharings.[2] These were contracts by which the king was associated with a local seigneur in the government of his demesne, thereby extending the king's direct influence over towns pertaining to a particular seigneur. Louis VI. created six such establishments, in Soisi, Montchauvet, Verrines, Boulai, Fossé des Champeaux à Paris and Fontenai.[3] In so doing, as in the case of the bailiffs, he simply anticipated Philip Augustus,[4] who extended Louis' associative government into points in Burgundy, Bourbon, Sancerre, Dreux, the bishoprics of Auxerre, Laon, Beauvais and elsewhere. The advantage of this copartnership was greater to the crown than to the local lord. The latter purchased royal protection by a partial sacrifice of independence and income. " Naturally they were usually resorted to by ecclesiastical establishments; but sharings between the king and lay vassals were not unknown. Though the small holder obtained protection and often an increase of privileges, by dividing the benefits of his fief with the king, the gain to the monarchy was even more. The partition was usually made on the basis of an equal division of the income, save that distinctively churchly impositions like tithes and certain portions of the church

et quos coeteri mei feodati, computavi nullum praetermittens," etc. (1125).— *Cartul. de Saint Denis*, t. I., p. 234.

[1] Les travaux administratifs de Suger auront pour premier théatre le temporel même de son abbaye; mais ils ne nous offriront pas moins un sujet d'observations intéressantes, puisque nous les verrons en suite servir de modèle pour l'administration même du royaume.—Huguenin, 32.

[2] "C'est Louis le Gros qui fonda, sur ce point comme sur tant d'autres, la tradition monarchique."—Luchaire, *Annales*, Introd., cxcvii. See also *Manuel*, 384, 415.

[3] Luchaire, *Annales*, Nos. 355, 403, 457, 492, 572, 597. On the character, importance and extension of the *pariages*, see Luchaire, *Inst. Mon.*, II., 195–201.

[4] Walker, 123.

lands or buildings, were reserved as the exclusive property of religious establishments. The administration was in the hands of officers chosen jointly by the monarch and the sharer, or, if not so chosen, bound by oath to each of the contracting parties. It is easy to see how such an arrangement would inure to the profit of a strong monarch, allowing him, as it did, to have control of the local administration of the fief and to use its fortifications in the interest of the crown."[1]

[1] Walker, 122-3.

CHAPTER VI.

RELATION OF LOUIS VI. TO THE CHURCH.

The fact that the reign of Louis VI. fell in the years immediately following the pontificate of Gregory VII., when the Clugny
reform movement was at its height, suggests the query, What
was the attitude of Louis towards the Church and the Holy
See ? The answer is of consequence in virtue of the light cast
upon the throne and its power.

In the process of feudalization to which all institutions succumbed in greater or less degree, the church had not escaped.
The life all round it was feudal, and there was thus a gradual
infiltration into the church of feudalizing elements. The church
in Gaul had suffered under the precarious condition of the government following the division of the empire. The decline, too,
was aggravated by the Norman incursions. The king, upon
whom hitherto the exercise of electoral power in the bishoprics
had depended, was obliged to divide with the lords. Feudal
pretensions invaded episcopal seats. In many dioceses count or
viscount controlled the elections[1] and appropriated church revenues to personal uses. Yet although the Carlovingians and Capetians had to share their influence in episcopal elections with
counts, or viscounts they contrived to retain a preponderant
influence. The king's ecclesiastical sovereignty, conveyed in
the term *regale* was never so divided as his political authority.[2]

[1] *Revue des Quest. Hist.*, Jan. 1894, p. 6. *L'Église au XIe siècle dans la
Gascogne.*

[2] This power, in the case of the king, no less than in that of the count,
extended beyond the rôle which ecclesiastical theory allowed, according to
which the king was the protector, not the proprietor of the church and its property. But in spite of protest the king continued to direct affairs (with the
qualifications mentioned on pp. 59–60.) *Rev. des Quest. Hist.*, Jan. 1894, p. 296.
Review of Imbart de la Tour's " *Les Élections épiscopales dans l'Église de France*

Some remnants of supremacy remained in localities not forming a portion of the royal domain, which were used to the advantage of the central power.[1] We have seen before this, what financial advantages regalian rights afforded the crown ; the political advantage was no less effective. "The right of regalia carried with it the privilege of appointing to the benefices ordinarily in the gift of the bishop ; thus allowing the king to fill these territories, often in the heart of the lay fiefs, with his partisans."[2] This extended also to the choice of the heads of numerous abbeys, which the interest of protection from the local nobles bound to the crown, and so emphasized the power of the crown in lay lands.[3] The king thus had a measure of power transcending his ordinary authority. In the time of Louis le Gros the circle of regalian influence was confined to northern and central France — the episcopate of Rheims, the province of Sens, Bourges, Champagne, Bourgogne, Nivernais, including Auxerre and Tonnerre, and Auvergne. In Normandy, in fiefs of the house of Anjou, in Flanders, Brittany, Toulouse, and the feudal group of the south, regalian rights fell to the crown[4] only by conquest or other annexa-

du IXᵉ au XIIᵉ siècles". The right, however, was subject to important variations. Before the Gregorian reform it was entire, wherever held. From that time it became more qualified, but through the partial failure of the reform, it was never seriously impaired. (See Luchaire, *Manuel*, § 276.) The letter of Suger, while regent (Duchesne, IV., 498), to the church of Chartres, is particularly clear in defining the *régale* : Sugerius Dei gratia B. Dionysii abbas, Capitulo Carnotensi, Roberto scilicet decano, et aliis, salutem et dilectionem. Quod unanimiter et communi pace pontificem vobis domnum Gostenum archidiaconum elegistis, valde nobis placet. . . . . Nos autem, quantum ex parte domini regis cujus vices agimus, facere habemus, huic electioni libenter assensum præbemus. De regalibus vero, sicut in curia Dominorum Regum Francorum mos antiquus fuisse dinoscitur, cum episcopus consecratus et in palatinum ex more canonico fuerit introductus, tunc reddentur omnia. Hic est enim redditionis ordo et consuetudo, ut, sicut diximus, in palatio statutus, regi et regno fidelitatem faciat, et sic, demum regalia recipiat.

[1] Clamageran, I., 276. *Cf.* H. F., XIV., liii.
[2] Walker, 99.
[3] For Louis VI.'s management of the royal abbeys see Luchaire, *Annales*, Introd., pp. cliv-vi.
[4] *Ibid.*, cviii-cxi. Brussel, I., 295-309.
Louis VI. allowed the privilege of election to remain to the bishoprics and

tions. Louis was jealous of the regalia[1] and kept a watchful eye upon appointments in bishopric or abbey.[2] In respect of this policy, Louis VI. predetermined the larger conduct of Philip Augustus.[3] Such rights, permeating where else the king could not enter, gave a solidity to the royal power not afforded in any other way.

It was inevitable where Church and State were so intimately connected, that there should be conflict between the ecclesiastical and secular powers; but in spite of the anathemas of the church, the *régale* triumphed.[4] In case of such union, the truest political science demanded that the state be paramount.[5] The idea of the state, as the idea of the nation, were both nascent

abbeys in Aquitaine and Poitiers. This was just before his death. The act sets forth in clear style the duties of royal power to the church : Regiæ majestatis est, ecclesiarum quieti pia sollicitudine providere ; et ex officio susceptæ a Domino pietatis earum libertatem tueri, et ab hostium seu malignantium incursibus defensare. Ea propter petitionibus vestris, communicato praesente episcoporum abbatuum et procerum nostrorum consilio, assentienti Ludovico filio nostro jam in regem sublimato, duximus annuemdum, et in sede Burdegalensi et in praenominatis episcopalibus sedibus, abbatiisque ejusdem provinciae quae, defuncto illustri Aquitanorum duce et comite Pictavis Guillelmo, per filiam ipsius Alienordim jam dicto filio nostro Ludovico forte matrimonii cedit, in episcoporum et abbatuum suorum electionibus canonicam omnino concedimus libertatem absque homini, juvamenti seu fidei per manum datae, obligatione. . . . . Hoc quoque adjicientes, ut omnes ecclesiae infra denominatam provinciam constitutae, praedia, possessiones ad ipsas jure pertinentia, secundum privilegia et justitias et bonas consuetudines suas, habeant et possideant illibita. quin ecclesiis ipsis universis et earum ministris, cum possessionibus suis, canonicam in omnibus concedimus libertatem.—Brussel, I., 286.

[1] " In dem hohen Masse, wie Ludwig dem Klerus gegenüber seine Pflichten als Schutzherr wahrnahm und demselben zahlreiche Beweise der Gunst gab, wahrte er streng die ihm zustehenden kirchlichen Rechte, besonders die sich auf die Regalien, sowie auf Wahl und Bestätigung der Bischöfe und Äbte beziehenden."— Hirsch, *Studien zur Geschichte König Ludwigs VII.*, p. 14.

[2] See the cases, Luchaire, *Annales*, Introd., clxix–clxx.

[3] Luchaire, *Ibid.*, Introd. p. clvi.

[4] Clamageran, I., 290.

[5] " The State is the public power, offensive and defensive, both at home and abroad. In the life of the State and of states, authority is thus the essential thing. . . . . Only the State has the duty or the right to be the authority in this sense. Wherever justice, property, society, *wherever even the church*, the

potentialities in France in the twelfth century, but the royal attitude of Louis was a valuable preparative to that discovery. When pontifical authority did not invade the palace, or oppose the ends of government, he was a ready supporter of Rome;[1] but he believed that France's interests were paramount.

This is made manifest in an occurrence of the year 1114. The diocese of Noyon was situated in that penumbral region between France and the empire. It was French in sentiment, while Tournai, in the same ecclesiastical department, inclined towards Germany. In 1114, on the death of the bishop, the two sections, each with its own candidate, struggled for the mastery. Pascal II. was favorable to a division of the diocese; but such a separation would deliver to Flanders and the county of Hainaut, and, perhaps, to the Empire, an area hitherto subject to the regalian jurisdiction of the king of France. Pascal went so far as to give to Tournai a special bishop, but Calixtus II., in 1121, owing to the strenuous efforts of Louis, reunited Tournai and Noyon.[2] The same question, in reverse manner, occurred again in 1124 when the pope sought to unite the bishophic of Arras to that of Cambrai. Again Louis VI. interposed and forced the pope to maintain Arras in his exclusive control. The union, if consummated, would have reduced the territory penetrated by the *regale*, and possible also have been a source of conflict with the Empire.[3] Motives of expediency constrained each party not to go to extremes. Necessity constrained Louis not to be too aggressive, and without doubt the support of the crown of France, indirect as it was, was of aid to the pope in his protracted struggle

people, or the community, come into the position of authority, the nature of the State is either not yet discovered or lost in degeneracy."—Droysen, *Principles of History* (Andrews' translation), p. 42.

[1] In 1112 Louis VI. writes to the pope : Ego Ludovicus . . . . praemunitus, dignum ac valde necessarium duximus, ut quando pontificalis auctoritas verbi gratia non praevalet, nostra potentia subministret ; et quod perfidorum violentia Deo militantibus subtrahitur nostre majestatis formidine ad ultimum reformetur. —Mabillon, 642.

[2] See Luchaire, *Annales*, No. 172, and Introd. cxxv.–cxxix. The confirmation of Calixtus is in Robert's *Bullaire*, No. 263. Eugenius III. later (1146) divided the diocese. (Luchaire, *Manuel*, 40, note.)

[3] On these two cases, see Luchaire, *Inst. Mon.*, II. 263–4 and notes.

with the empire.[1] The pope dared not go to extremes lest the conflict between the papacy and the empire be repeated in Gaul.[2]

The history of royal justice under Louis VI., so far as the relations of the court of the king to ecclesiastical matters is concerned, is one of great obscurity. There is no reason to believe, however, that in asserting the competence of his court over things pertaining to the church he abated his claims.[3] Louis adhered to—even strengthened—whatever legal or customary

---

[1] Aside from the dynastic tie which bound the emperor to the foe of the French king, between the two powers east and west of the Rhine, there could not be any pacific feeling. The French king enjoyed in comparative security the right for which the emperor was struggling and which he was obliged partially to surrender by the Concordat of Worms (1122). This jealousy was aggravated, too, because French influence had been exerted in favor of the pope, the emperor's mortal enemy, although in the nature of things Louis VI. could derive no advantage from his conduct, even though Calixtus II. were his uncle. "Das Schisma welches Heinrich vor drei Jahren erneuert hatte, war ein trauriger Anachronismus gewasen, dessen Wirkungen er selbst ubel genug empfand; das Abendland ertrug keinen Papst mehr, der sich lediglich auf die Macht des Kaisers stutzte. Darauf beruhte zuletzt der vollstandige Sieg des Calix, eine wie bedeutende Hülfe ihm auch sein koniglicher Neffe in Frankreich gewahrt hatte. Es lag nur in der Natur der Dinge dass sich Konig Ludwig für die geleisteten Dienste schlecht belohnt glaubte, als der Pabst nicht mehr in alle seine Forderungen willigte, und dass dieser dagegen sich solchen Undank wenig zu Hertzen nahm. Er wollte so wenig ein Vassall Frankreichs, wie des deutchen Kaisers, sondern das freie Oberhaupt der Kirche sein—und war es."—Giesebrecht, III., 930.

[2] Ives of Chartres writes (1113): Quod ergo hactenus cum pace et utilitate ecclesiae observatum est, humiliter petimus ut de coetero observatur, et regni Francorum pax et summi sacerdotii nulla subreptione dissolvatur. Quod idcirco praelibamus quia audivimus clericos Tornacenses ad apostolicam sedem venisse, petituros ut apostolica proeceptione proprium possint habere episcopum, et Noviomensis ecclesiae frustrare privilegium. Quod ne fiat sicut filii et fideles rogamus et consulimus ; . . . . *ne hac occasione schisma quod est in Germanico regno adversus sedem apostolicam in Galliarum regno suscitetis* . . . . Tornacensibus non esse dandum proprium episcopum, ne in offen sam regis Francorum incurrat.—H. F., XV., 160.

[3] The principle of the superiority of the justice of the state over that of the church is clearly set forth in the act of partition of the *banlieue* between Louis VI. and the bishop of Paris (1112–1116). See Luchaire, *Annales*, Introd. clviii., and No. 218 ; Tardif, No. 345 ; Guérard, *Cartul. de Notre-Dame de Paris*, I., 252.

prerogatives attended the king's office.   The church, while quite willing in case of need to be plaintiff in the royal court, had before Louis' time assumed, with admirable inconsistency, to try in its own courts all cases wherein an ecclesiastic was the defendant.[1] This invasion of the competence of the king's court by the hierarchy, while never reaching the point attained by the seigneurial power,[2] was quite general in the later eleventh century — that is to say, in the times of the magnificent papal pretensions of Gregory VII.   In 1093 Ives of Chartres, the great advocate of the Clugny reform, replied to a summons of the royal court, — "*in ecclesia, si ecclesiastica sunt negotia; vel in curia, si sunt curialia,*" — language guarded enough for any reservation he might choose to make.[3]   Filled with cloud-capped ideas of the eminence of the church, the bishop of Chartres sought to make the prevots of his diocese[4] address themselves to Rome instead of appealing, as they naturally did, to the justice of the king.[5]   But he was to live to learn that the little finger of Louis VI. was as thick as his father's thigh.   He could not dispose of a summons of Louis VI. by a stroke of the pen.   In 1114 a chevalier of Beauvais was killed, through the instigation of a canon. The cathedral chapter at once took the matter in hand, and denied the cognizance of the royal tribunal, although the action was criminal, on the ground that the chapter alone was competent to try its members.   In this the canons were sustained by Ives, the bishop of Chartres, who at the same time

[1] Luchaire, *Manuel*, 557.

[2] Pardessus, 4, 5.

[3] See Luchaire, *Inst. Mon.*, I., 295.   There are two monographs pertaining to this subject : Sieber, *Bischof Ivo von Chartres und seine Stellung zu den kirchenpolitischen Fragen seine Zeit;*   Theil, *Die politische Thatigkeit des Abtes Bernhard von Clairvaux.*

[4] "Accusavit (Ivo) enim nos " writes one of the prevots, "dicens quod regem adissemus, regem in rebus ecclesiae nostrae manum mittere fecissemus.   Itaque orasse ad vestrum auxilium et consilium confugisse nunc nobis nocet.   Nunc enim nobis jus et negavit, et negat, et Romam invito nos trahit et invitat."— *Bibl. de l'Ecole des Chartes*, 1855 ; L. Merlet, *Lettres de Ivo de Chartres*, pp. 449–450.   Quoted in Luchaire, *Inst. Mon.*, I., 295, note 2.

[5] The lesser clergy were far more in consonance with the policy of the crown than high prelates.

indulged in the melancholy reflection that if the chapter renounced its competence, it violated the canon law; while if it refused, it incurred the wrath of the king (*si audientiam regalis curiae respuitis, regem offenditis*). Louis VI. had the murderer arrested; the clerical party replied by laying Beauvais under interdict.[1] We are ignorant of the issue of the struggle; the canon may have escaped severe punishment, owing to the protraction of the struggle;[2] or the chapter may have purchased permission to try the cause, as in the case of Gaudri, the bishop of Laon.[3] In the light of Louis' policy, however, it is hard to believe that the crown retreated from its position.

The period between 1126 and 1135 is signalized by the further struggle of Louis with the clergy of reform. Louis VI. had no intention of abandoning to papal control a prerogative so valuable as that of the *regale*. Rome and the reforming party had triumphed at Rheims in 1106,[4] but the responsibility of government was then not all Louis' own. As king, Louis was determined to control the *regale* in spite of the protests of Rome. Aside from the advantage to the crown from the right of investiture in lay fiefs, the crown had been accustomed to use the church in other capacities. Hence he regarded the new propaganda as inimical to the interests of monarchy. The vice of feudalism was its separativeness. Investiture was the only means of contact which the king had with many fiefs. Louis was

[1] See H. F., XV., 168–70; Letters of Ives of Chartres, Nos, 137, 263, 264; Guibert de Nogent, I., chap. xvii.; Luchaire, *Annales*, No. 174; *Inst. Mon.*, I., 297–8; Guizot, *Civilization in France*, Course IV., Lect. 4; *Revue Hist.* (1890), Vol. XLII., p. 87; Langlois, *Les Origines du Parlement de Paris.*.

[2] This is the hypothesis of M. Guizot.

[3] In 1110 Gerard de Quierzi was assassinated by accomplices of Gaudri, bishop of Laon, then at Rome. The royal prévot in the city at once called upon the bourgeois, burned the houses of the conspirators, and drove them out of the city. The king knowing that the bishop was the instigator of the murder, confiscated his property and forbade him his episcopal duties. Gaudri, meanwhile, had returned from Rome with letters of absolution from the pope. Louis, however, persisted in his attitude, and Gaudri was only allowed to assume his place on payment of money.—*Annales*, No. 93; H. F., XII., 246–9. *Cf.* No. 518.

[4] Luchaire, *Annales*, clvi. ff.; Imbart de la Tour, *Les Élections épiscopales*, pp. 356–7.

not an enemy of reform. His attitude in this matter has been
misunderstood. He has been accused of deliberate persecution
of the church;[1] whereas his sole purpose was to establish the
precedence of the state in matters pertaining to church *and* state.[2]
Effective reform had to proceed from the government; this Louis
VI. saw; he could not abandon the cardinal principles of his policy.[3] Fortunately Suger, as Stephen de Garland before him, was
wise enough to see the wisdom of this course. Although he
refused to wear a secular title, Suger nevertheless preserved in
his spiritual discipline an active participation in temporal affairs.
He was no less a man of the church for that he had a vivid interest in things of the world; he saw with rare insight the necessity
of coöperation between the two greatest forces of the time.

The moral situation between the king and the party of reform
was sometimes serious.[4] Against the monarchy was the clergy of
the Ile-de-France, with the order of Citeaux, and the foremost
advocate of church authority in Europe, Bernard of Clairvaux.

[1] Combes, 22. St. Bernard called him "a second Herod."—H. F., XV., 548.

[2] Louis VI. proved the sincerity of his intentions by taking Clugny under
special protection.—Luchaire, *Annales*, No. 276.

[3] Louis le Gros in granting a charter to the church of St. Cornelius, at
Compiègne, felt it necessary to accompany the privileges bestowed with a
restriction worded as though it were a novelty, to the effect that those in holy
orders, connected with the foundation, should have no wives—a condition
which shows how little confidence existed in the mind of the sagacious prince
as to the efficacy of the canons so pretentiously promulgated. "Ut clerici ejusdem
ecclesiae sicut usque modo vixerunt permaneant; hoc tamen praecipimus ut
presbyteri, diaconi, subdiaconi, nulla tenus deinceps uxores concubinas habeant;
cæteri vero cujuscumque ordinis clerici propter fornicationem, licentiam habeant
ducendi uxores."—DuCange, *Concubina*. Cited in Lea, *Hist. Sacerdotal Celibacy*, p. 270. "The correspondence of Ives of Chartres is a sufficient confes-
sion of the utter futility of the ceaseless exertions which for half a century the
church had been making to enforce her discipline." Lea, p. 263. See Letters,
Nos. 200, 218, 277.

[4] See the conflict of Louis VI. with the archbishop of Sens (Luchaire,
Annales, No. 448); with the bishop of Paris (*Ibid.*, Nos. 424, 427–8, 439, 465); with
Hildebert of Tours (*Ibid.*, Nos. 367, 400, 426, 432, 460, 473). On the contest
over investitures, with Pascal II. consult *Acad. des Inscript.*, VI., 565 (1819). A
detailed account of Louis VI.'s relations with the episcopate is in Luchaire,
Annales, Introd., pp. cliii–clxxviii.

The terrible struggle between the king and the bishop of Paris ended in the capitulation of the partisans of the Clugny propaganda, while that with Hildebert of Tours ended in the complete surrender of Hildebert. When it was at last understood that the royal power would brook no reduction of its authority, conveyed either in law or precedent, church and state profited alike. Louis VI.'s wise policy of moderation when contrasted with the drastic policy of Henry III. in Germany,[1] spared France the conflict which sundered the Empire. The question of investiture — the cardinal principle of the Clugny reform — never reached the stupendous proportions in France that it attained in Germany and Italy, or even in England.

The silence of the French chronicles regarding the matter is significant. Neither in charters, nor in pontifical letters, nor in the writers of the period, is there allusion to any agreement concluded between the monarchy and the papacy, like the Concordat of Worms (1122) in Germany, or the settlement made between the English king and the pope in 1107. The council of Rheims (October 20, 1119) under Calixtus II. was the last synod held in France in which the question of investiture was agitated.[2] Calixtus was a violent fanatic and intended to promulgate a general interdict, but the temper of the assembly obliged him to modify the decree.[3] It is probable that from this time forth the kings ceased gradually to give investiture by ring and crosier before consecration, without submitting to this concession by official declaration or public act. The truth is that from the reign of Louis VI. it can be said that the crown ceased to insist on its direct right of nomination allowing a measure of local liberty in the election of bishops.[4] The king trusted the Gallican clergy, and on the whole their sentiments of loyalty and independence warranted that trust.[5]

[1] See this dissertation, introd., p. 8.

[2] On this council consult Freeman's *Norman Conquest*, V. 189–91, or Robert *Calixte* II., ch. vi.

[3] Imbart de la Tour.—*Les Élections épiscopales*, p. 398 and note 1.

[4] *Ibid.*, p. 399.

[5] Thus in 1137 Louis granted liberty of episcopal elections to the churches

That the reconciliation between the king and the church party was real and complete,[1] an event of the year 1130 furnishes proof. After the death of Honorius II. the Christian world was divided in the question whether the claims of Innocent II. or those of Anacletus should have preferment. Louis VI. convened a council at Étampes. Among the prelates came St. Bernard and Hildebert the penitent archbishop of Tours. The king appealed to Bernard to decide, for he had but to open his mouth and the Spirit gave him utterance.[2] His decision given in favor of Innocent was considered the judgment of God. In the nature of things, Louis secured no direct results at this time. Whatever important aid the king of France had given Innocent, the pope was willing to be a vassal of the king of France as little as of the emperor. He wanted to be the free head of the church, and he was, but the indirect effect to France, in the prestige given the monarchy, in the eyes of Europe, was not inconsiderable, Germany and England followed France and also recognized Innocent II. as pope.

Meanwhile the king and his minister had begun the work of reforming the monasteries. Corruption and debauchery ruled, even in St. Denis,[3] and also in its priory of Argen-

of Aquitaine, but the privilege was not accorded at the demand of the pope nor was it owing even to the initiative of local seigneurs. Luchaire, *Annales*, No. 581.

[1] Stephen, the bishop of Paris, attended Louis VI., in his last hours.— Suger, 129.

[2] "Aperuit os suum et Spiritus Sanctus implevit illud."—*Ex vita sancti Bernardi*, H. F., XIV., 364. On this schism see Suger, 118; *Chron. Maurin.*, H. F., XII., 79; *Ex actis sanctorum et illustrium virorum gestis*, H. F., XIV., 256. Luchaire, *Annales*, No. 460, has a valuable note.

[3] Antiqua religio non parum in eodem monasterio refriguerat, extēriores quoque possessiones paulatim diminutae erant, sed et nonnulla sinistrae famae de eisdem virginibus dicebantur. Unde multum contristatus idem pontifex . . . . consilio et auctoritate domini Papae Innocentii, dominique Renaldi Remorum archiepiscopi, Ludovici quoque regis Francorum, ad quem eadem ecclesiae proprie pertinere dicebatur, omnes pariter illas sanctimoniales ex illa ejecit.—H. F., XIV., 348, *Gesta Bartholomaei Laudunensis episcopi. Cf.* Letter of Louis VI. Gall. Christ. IX., col. 192.

In ecclesia sancti Dionysii, Parisiensis diocesis, reformatur religio per industriam et bonum propositum Sugerii, ejusdem loci abbatis. Nam per negli-

teuil.[1] Suger effectively renovated many places,[2] not only reforming the moral life of the monks, but their temporal condition as
well. In the priories of St. Denis he revised the method of government, requiring ecclesiastical prevots to have a knowledge of the
law, a qualification hitherto unheard of. He induced the king
to relieve the inhabitants of the *ville* of St. Denis of the right of
mortmain; he redeemed the *octrois*, repurchased rights which
had become alienated or usurped, and by planting vineyards and
orchards, advanced the temporal interests of the people.[3] In
the light of the numerous concessions made by Louis VI. to
abbeys and churches,[4] or the confirmation of donations or
exemptions made by former kings,[5] or by local seigneurs,[6] it
is difficult to think of him otherwise than as a patron of the
church. But Louis VI. was not prompted by humanitarian
motives, in doing as he did, so much as by material results
derived by the crown from the increased worth of his people,
else he would have abolished the barbarous right of spoil,[7] by

gentiam abbatuum et quorumdam illius ecclesiae monachorum regularis instituto,
ita ab eodem loco abjecta erat, quod, vix speciem vel habitum religionis prae-
tendebant monachis."—Guil. de Nangis, p. 13. (*Société de l'Histoire de France.*)

[1] Suger, 100. *Œuvres de Suger* (*Administration Abbatiale*), Edition of Lecoy
de la Marche, 160–1, and *Éclaircissements*, 441.

[2] Luchaire, *Annales*, Nos. 410, 413, 431, 433, 519, 565. Suger's own account
of the reform of St. Denis is in Suger, 95–99. In. *Chron. Maurin*, H. F., XII.,
78 there is a good description of an investigation, showing the hostility of the
monks.

[3] Huguenin, 27–30. The charter of Louis VI. is in Duchesne, IV., 548,
and in translation in Combes, *Pièces Justificatives*, No. 4, p. 310.

[4] Luchaire, *Annales*, Nos. 52, 58, 65, 66, 69, 86, 98, 100, 107, 141, 151, 163,
171, 173, 193, 194, 196, 204, 206, 224, 225, 234, 241, 250, 271, 274, 278, 284, 286,
289, 293, 329, 342, 354, 361, 363, 397, 419, 442, 453, 464, 477, 479, 482, 483, 495,
498, 503, 517, 522, 535, 537, 538, 539, 541, 543, 550, 574, 591, 592, 593, 596, 606,
615, 616, 619–22, 631, 634, 636.

[5] Luchaire, *Annales*, Nos. 140, 144, 148, 195, 292, 294, 302, 323, 324, 326,
332, 350, 370, 501, 504, 507, 513, 532, 534, 536, 557, 633.

[6] *Ibid.*, Nos. 101, 104, 112, 115, 126, 232, 235, 251, 283, 304, 306, 319, 320,
329, 346, 347, 352, 354, 357, 364, 366, 368, 436, 447, 457, 458, 485, 514, 515, 528,
548, 561, 599, 604, 635, 637, 638.

[7] H. F., XV., 341. Luchaire, *Manuel*, 49. For the abolition of this abuse
by Louis VII., see *Inst. Mon.*, II., 66–7.

which the king took to himself the goods and revenues of a deceased prelate.   Motives of expediency to the king were more urgent than graces of charity were attractive.[1]

[1] This is far from asserting, however, that Louis VI. was deficient in kindness of heart.   On the contrary he was beloved by his friends and the common folk. Suger's account shows that the king was genuinely loved by his people:—Cum autem paulatim ad incolumitatem respiraret, quo potuit vehiculo prope Milidunum ad fluvium Sequane, occurentibus et concurrentibus per viam ei obviam et Deo personam ejus commendantibus a castellis et vicis et relictis aratris devotissimis populis quibus pacem conservaverat, etc.   Suger, p. 127.

CHAPTER VII.

KING AND COMMUNES. ROYALTY AND THE POPULAR CLASSES.

From the time of Louis VI. the emancipation of the serf ceases to be a religious sentiment of sporadic growth, and becomes a conscious policy of the crown[1] that contributed to the increase of the royal power of the crown, in weakening feudal customs and in the consequent economic and social elevation of the people. The direct purpose of Louis, however, was not so much to elevate the serf as to humble the barons. Owing to Suger's careful management, to the king power was more to be desired than riches. Yet Louis was far from displaying indifference to the acquisition of wealth. His cupidity was notorious. Nothing can equal the cynicism which he displayed in the sale of the charter of the commune of Laon,[2] yet there must have been some promptings of heart in the act of Louis which permitted a freeman to marry a serf without losing his liberty.[3] There were several ways in which manumission could be effected. Sometimes the servile condition was ameliorated by converting men of the church into men of the king,[4] or by placing ordinary serfs in the custody of the church.[5] Sometimes an abbot, as that of St. Denis, was given the right of manumission without seeking royal

[1] Luchaire, *Manuel*, 380.

[2] See this dissertation, p. 88, n. 2, and on the avarice of Louis VI. in general. Luchaire *Annales*, Introd., pp. xxxv–xxxvi.

[3] Tardif, No. 392.

[4] Luchaire, *Annales*, No. 41.

[5] Luchaire, *Annales*, 482. Ecclesiastical serfs were superior in point of advantage to common serfs. (Luchaire, *Manuel*, 310.) Pascal II. in 1114 wrote to Galon of Paris : Neque enim aequum est ecclesiasticam familiam iisdem conditionibus coerceri, quibus servi saecularium hominum coercerentur.— Guerard, *Cartul. de Notre-Dame de Paris*, I. 223. On the other hand, royal serfs were still better off. (Luchaire, *Manuel*, 312).

authorization.[1]   In St. Denis, St. Quentin, Soissons, Laon, and Orleans, the king also abolished the right of mortmain for all persons above seven years of age.[2] However, in such emancipations and exemptions, he had too much sagacity to go to extremes. The prohibition imposed upon enfranchised serfs of Laon by which they were prevented from evading military service by entering the ranks of the clergy, the chevalerie, or the bourgeois, is a clear enunciation of the principle that those indebted to the king are expected to do the king's business.[3] Thus it was no unusual thing to find men of low birth, in his reign, figuring not without honor in the host.[4]

Louis endeavored to promote centers of population and agriculture by means of assurances of protection, exemption for a term of years, and by franchises and liberties. This fact is attested by numerous ordinances. The cases of Touri,[5] Beaune-la-Rolande,[6] Augere Regis,[7] and Etampes,[8] which were repopulated and restored to a prosperous condition, are in point.

The most notable instance of such restoration, however, is the case of Lorris, in Gâtanais, at once one of the most fertile and yet the most harassed of the departments of the Ile de France. Its constitution was widely imitated in the twelfth and thirteenth cen-

[1] Luchaire, *Annales*, No. 144. Decrevimus etiam et statuimus, et regio edicto praecepimus, ut abhas et monachi sancti Dyonisii sociorum ejus plenam, habeant potestatem de servis et ancillis ecclesie emancipandis, et liberos faciendi, consilio capituli sui, non requisito assensu vel consilio nostro.—Tardif, No. 347. *Cf.* Luchaire, *Annales*, No. 160, Abbey of Chalons-sur-Marne.

[2] Combes, 62, and notes. Louis VII. made the abolition entire.—Luchaire, *Études sur les Actes de Louis VII.* Paris, 1885. No. 15.

[3] Ego Ludovicus . . . notum fieri volumus, quod homines isti sive mulieres, quorum nomina subscribuntur, liberi servientes nostri sunt et licentur ad clericatum sive miliciam et ad communionem, sive contradictione, possunt assumi . . . Masculi vero, exceptis clericis, militibus aut in communione manentibus, nisi morbo vel senio graventur, expediciones nostras bannales debent, si submonit, fiunt.—Luchaire, *Annales*, Textes Inedits, p. 337–8.

[4] Vuitry, I. 377, n. 3.

[5] Luchaire, *Annales*, No. 237.

[6] *Ibid.*, No. 165.

[7] *Ibid.*, No. 273.

[8] *Ibid.*, No. 333. On this work of Louis VI., see Luchaire, *Annales*, introd., clxxxii–cxci. More than fifty acts of privilege are recorded of him.

turies.[1] Out of the depths of the feudal age the customs of Lorris reveal in a remarkable manner the purposes and teachings of a broader and more expansive era.   The inhabitant of Lorris paid only the nominal sum of six *derniers* for his house and each acre of land which he possessed.[2]   In the radius of Étampes, Orleans and Melun, *tailles*, *corvees*, gifts and the like were abolished[3] and the peasant was entitled to enjoy without molestation the fruits of his labors.[4] Commerce was protected; purchase and sale were without restraint[5] The use of the oven in Lorris was free.[6] The tax on salt was reduced to one *dernier* per cart load.[7] Military service was for a day at a time only.[8] Allowance was made for a liberal process of law, in that fines formerly of sixty *sous* were reduced to five, and those of five *sous* were reduced to twelve *derniers*.[9] Resort to law could be avoided by accommodation,[10] the manifest intention being to make appeal to arms of rare recourse.[11] But the assurances of civil liberty were perhaps the most phenomenal provisions of these customs.   Article 8 provided that no man of Lorris should be obliged to go out of the *banlieue* to plead before the king — an example of the principle of "justice at home" which paved the way for a provision which is certainly not remote from the right of *habeas corpus*. "No one," runs article 16, "shall be detained in prison if he can furnish bail for his appearance in court."

The charter of Lorris found a ready acceptance elsewhere : in Corcelles-le-Roi, Saint Michel, Breteau near Auxerre, La

---

[1] The history of the Customs of Lorris is shrouded in obscurity; but the fact that Louis VI. has the honor to have instituted them is no longer in doubt, although the date of their establishment is not known. No document of Louis VI. exists, but the customs are attested by a confirmation (1155) of Louis VII. (Luchaire, *Catal.*, No. 351) and another by Philip Augustus in 1187. (Delisle, *Études sur les actes de Phillippe-Auguste*, No. 187). See Prou: "*Les Coutumes de Lorris et leur propagation aux XIIe et XIIIe siècles*" *Nouvelle Revue historique de droit français et étranger*, VIII. (1884), pp. 139, 267, 441. Viollet *Hist. du Droit français*, 116.

[2] Art. 1.	[6] Art. 24.	[10] Art. 12.
[3] Arts. 4 and 5.	[7] Art. 26.	[11] Art. 14.
[4] Art. 2.	[8] Art. 3.	
[5] Arts. 16 and 17.	[9] Art. 7.	

Brosse in the diocese of Sens, in Le Moulinet and La Chapelle-le-Reine, in Barville, Batilly, Loup - des - Vignes, Villeneuve-le-roi, Montargis, Voisines, Cléry and other places.[1] The uniformity of the customs thus inspired by Louis le Gros and continued by Louis VII. and Philip Augustus must have produced, in a sense, a solidarity not otherwise to be attained.[2] Other grants of privilege to places or persons, further attest Louis' deliberate efforts to break the iron grip of feudalism.[3] But such qualified privileges would have contributed only slightly to the progress of liberty if the movement had not found in the communes centers of aggressive agitation.

The spell which feudalism and the church had conspired to cast over Europe was now broken by the rise of the cities. The strength of conscious power in the hearts of the burgher class, united with that solidarity which common interests imparted, now gave birth to what Europe had not known for centuries — the people. Europe had known men, but the vital energy of a popular spirit had been lost since the second decline of imperial rights in the west.

It is not in the province of this dissertation to enter into a study of the origin of the mediæval communes. Whether their germ be found in the revivification of latent Roman municipal survivals; or in the assertion of Germanic traditions, not lost, but dormant; whether guild corporations of merchants or craftsmen be responsible for the new life, or whether the initial impulse be found in some religious order, is not germane.[4] It is futile to try to identify the origin of the communes with any one form, nor will any collocation of these four elements explain

---

[1] *Ordonnances*, t. VIII, p. 500 ; Viollet, 116, citing Warkönig *Histoire de la Flandre*, I. 305. The text of the Customs of Lorris may be found in the *Ordonnances*, t. XI. pp. 200–203, in Prou, p. 125 ff. of the book form edition. An English translation is in Guizot, *Hist. of Civilization in France*, Course IV. Lect. 17.

[2] Combes, 300.

[3] Luchaire, *Annales*, Nos. 100, 102, 123, 197, 198, 237, 244, 551, 553, 554, 555, 576, 586, 600, 608, 611, 612.

[4] Luchaire, *Inst. Mon.*, II., 159 ff. has a terse presentation of the various theories of origin.

the uprising. The fact remains that the class of simple freemen who had disappeared in the ninth century, but the nature and condition of whose occupation had prevented them from being as tightly drawn into the feudal toils as others, come to light in the eleventh, and in the twelfth achieve political recognition. That the charters of the communes had for their prime object the restriction of the taxing power of the seigneur; that their magistracy derived its numbers and attributes largely from previous association; that the fragments of customary law found in the charters point to Germanic origin; that the communes of the twelfth century were aristocratic rather than democratic—these are the only statements which may be safely predicated.[1]

Leaving aside then the question of origins, a prime condition for communal life certainly existed in the local contiguity of those dwelling within walls. It was in many cases, we may believe, also an active cause, as much as the guild or religious associations. For it was natural that these communities, though governed entirely from without, should yet acquire some solidarity based on common interests. The ability to create wealth led the third estate inevitably to devise means to preserve wealth. Association, the only recourse of the weak, was the bar set against feudal arbitrariness.[2] Beside, there was an actual economic need. The townsmen demanded protection against the exactions of the clergy and the nobility. The event of first-rate importance in bringing about this political renaissance, was the invasions of the Northmen.[3] The cities, roused from their lethargy of four centuries

[1] Giry, *Établissments de Rouen*, I., 481.

[2] Compare the Carlovingian legislation against the *conjurationes*, true forerunners of the later efforts towards a more perfect union.—Waitz, IV., 362–4.

[3] The incursions of the Northmen had been a prime cause of the erection of castles. (Tunc quoque domus ecclesiarum per Gallias universas, praeter quas municipia civitatum velcastrorum servaverunt, etc.—Rod. Glaber, 19. *Collection de .Textes de la Société de l'École des Chartes. Cf.* the edict of Pistés, 864, of Charles the Bald. *De pace in Regno stabilienda, postscriptum* I. in Walter, *Corpus Juris Germanici antiqui* III., 156–7. Berlin, 1824.) In mediæval MSS. *municipium* is often used in the sense of castle (Suger, 10, 44 and n. 1). Sometimes *castrum, castellum* or *burgus* appear in the same sense. (Galbert de Bruges, cc. ix., xxviii. Jean d'Ypres, in *Mon. Germ. hist.* Script., xxv., 768). The agglomerated population under the walls of the *chateau* was

and forced to take vigorous and concerted action, acquired a unity not afterwards lost.   This unity brought with it a consciousness of power, and from this period on we find in the scant records remaining not a few instances of rebellion against count or bishop.   The Peasants' Revolt[1] in Normandy in 997, whether or not it affected the cities directly, at least shows the prevalence of the spirit.   At Cambrai, as early as 957, the townsmen shut the gates against their bishop;[2] Beauvais rose in 1074 and the men of Rheims in 1082.[3]   Le Mans was crushed with frightful severity in 1073,[4] but in Amiens the revolution was so firmly planted that in 1091 it was able to conclude an alliance with the Count of Flanders.[5]   In 1114 (or 1116) Angers in Anjou burst forth;[6] Lille and St. Omer in Flanders, in 1127,[7] and so the list grows longer and the circle widens as the years of revolution pass.

It is usual to say that the Crusades were a prime cause of the rise of the communes.   But we have seen above that Cambrai, Beauvais, Rheims, Le Mans and Amiens, in the region of the North alone, not to speak of others elsewhere, had reached the term of communal individuality before the first crusade.   In other words, the commune existed as a *de facto* institution before the Crusades began.   The moral fact inherent in the rise of the communes has been lost sight of in the dazzle and glitter of arms, attendant upon the Crusades.   The struggle of the mediæval communes in France, quite as much as in Lombard Italy, was the struggle for an idea really greater than the idea which animated the crusading movement.   The Crusades plunged Europe into three centuries of rapine and slaughter — into a warfare in which not

called *suburbani* (Galbert de Burges, c. ix.) who became the bourgeois of the communal epoch.   (*Ibid.*, cc. ix., xxviii.   *Cf.* the Charters of St. Omer of 1127, 1128.)

[1] See Freeman's *Norman Conquest*, I., 256–7.
[2] Brentano, 31.
[3] Luchaire, *Inst. Mon.*, II. 158, note.
[4] Freeman's *Norman Conquest*, IV., 550–1.
[5] Wauters, *Les libertés communales*, I., 365 ff.
[6] Norgate, *England under the Angevins*, I., 234–5.
[7] Hermann de Tournai, *M. G. H. SS.*, XIV., 289.

only men and women but thousands of children, too, were sacrificed for a purpose less worthy than that which characterized the warfare which racked Europe in the centuries following the second decline of imperial rights in the West. The conflict of pope and emperor, of emperor and Lombard cities, the wars of Otto I. and Henry III. with the great ducal houses, the Norman Conquest, the struggle between the Angevins and the French kings, all these were wars for real or fancied rights more real, more legitimate and less fanciful than were the wars of the Crusades. Crusading degenerated into a brilliant folly like that of tourneying, because the idea was too vague, the legitimacy of the movement too doubtful. The idea was mystical, even as its great preacher, St. Bernard, was a mystic. No one needs to be told that the results of the Crusades were far different from the intentions of their promoters: "Increasing at first the power of the popes and the Roman hierarchy, they tended at last to impair and diminish it. Expected to knit together the Latin and Greek churches, they made their divisions wider and added a feeling of exacerbation to their mutual relations. Intended to destroy forever Mahometan power in the East, they really contributed to strengthen it. Undertaken as a religious war to propagate the faith of Christ with the sword of Mahomet, and to vindicate Christian dogma against unbelievers, they really subserved the interests of free thought."[1] But apart from these wholly unforeseen and anomalous results, the Crusades were less fruitful of good effects than generally believed. The political results to Europe were slight.[2] Moreover, the economic results were quite as much a cause. Events are formative or resultant in their character according to the point of view, but in the study of history the point of view is *the* point quite as much as the thing seen from it. In measuring their effects, the Crusades must be taken as a whole. Their results were the results of a cumulative movement. It is quite impossible to posit definite effects to any one of them; how little, then, can be positively

[1] Owen, *Skeptics of the Italian Renaissance*, p. 24.

[2] Green, *Short History of the English People*, does not mention the crusades, except the incidental fact that Richard I. was a leader of the second crusade.

predicated as to the effects of the movement upon France in the twelfth century when the Crusades were yet in their beginning?

If it is impossible to distinguish with precision between the civilization sprung of the Crusades as a European movement and that which might have occurred without them, it is more impossible to ascribe any but the vaguest and slightest results which might have accrued from them to France in the reign of Louis VI. Mere absence from home of the barons was, I am inclined to believe, the most advantage derived by Louis VI. from this great European movement. The fighting instinct born in the blood and transmitted through two centuries of private warfare, denied expression at home, owing to the Truce of God and the vigor of the king,[1] sought relief in foreign war. The well-known letter of Suger[2] to Louis VII. is evidence that France felt the peace secured by the absence of turbulent barons more than anything else. The Crusades, in their inception, were a class movement, planned by princes and barons. They had little of the vital energy of a popular spirit. The people were more concerned in seeing the despoilers of their peace going away than in going themselves. After the first flush of triumph which followed the capture of Jerusalem, Europe again became absorbed in the nearer and keener struggle of emperor and pope. Men settled back into the old lines. When Edessa fell, the work-a-day world had almost forgotten that there was such a Christian outpost in Palestine. The shock of startled surprise that thrilled Europe when Edessa was taken is proof positive of how slight was the permanent effect which the first Crusade had exercised upon the mind of Europe in the twelfth century.

Having thus considered the origins of the communal movement, so far as necessary, it remains to inquire into the essential feature of the mediæval French commune. The essential elements of a commune were, first, an association confirmed by a charter; second, a code of fixed and sanctioned cus-

---

[1] According to Rambaud, *Civilisation française*, Vol. I., p. 224, Louis IX., in establishing the *Quarantaine-le-Roi*, simply revived an ordinance of Louis VI.

[2] H. F., XV., 509.

toms; third, a series of privileges which always included municipal or elective government.[1] The charter was at once a feudal title and a scheme of government. The principle that the commune had no right to exist without its charter was an invariable rule of the early period of the communal era.[2] The commune was, therefore, a sort of *petit état*. Yet no city of France ever achieved the republican freedom of Florence or Venice; no French king ever tolerated such municipal autonomy as the emperor was forced to abide in Lombard Italy.[3] Orleans, the only one which tried to make itself a commune in the highest sense, was crushed.[4]

The ancient legend that Louis VI. was the founder[5] of the communes is as untrue as the statement that he was their direct enemy.[6] The documentary history of the early communal epoch

[1] Brequigny, *Ordonnances*, XI., Introd. vii.

[2] Luchaire, *Manuel*, 414.

[3] Freeman's *Norman Conquest*, IV., 349.

[4] By Louis VII. H. F., XII., 196; *Hist. du Roi Louis VII.*, c. i. See Luchaire, *Inst. Mon.*, II., 170.

[5] Brussel, I., 178. Such categorical statements as that are not uncommon among the early historians. The *Charte* of 1814 will be remembered to have given this statement royal dress. A singular feature must be noticed here: It is the common belief that communal privileges were granted the bourgeois by the king, in order to relieve his subjects of grievous exactions, or at least prevent such exactions from being wholly empirical. If this were so it ought to follow that the communes be started in places where feudal oppressions were worst; whereas we find many of those recognized by Louis le Gros in fiefs of the church. Half the communes known to owe their foundation to him are so situated — Noyon, Beauvais, Soissons, Saint-Riquier, Corbie. (This enumeration does not include Laon, Amiens, or Bruyères-sous-Laon, where money figured as the prime motive.) Now the condition of serfs bound to the church glebe was better than average. (See this dissertation, p. 75, n. 5.) What is the conclusion? The bishops were an urban, the nobles a rural, aristocracy; in the cities popular feeling was rife, and Louis VI. saw in them points of resistance to the prevailing régime. This fact to me is luminous, for it shows that *he did more than let the movement merely take its course*. M. Dareste comes very near to the truth when he says: "L'erreur si longtemps accréditée, qui attribuait à la royauté l'initiative de la révolution communale, peut s'expliquer par le fait de son intervention progressive dans le gouvernement des villes."—*L'Administration de la France*. I., 173.

[6] Giry, *Établissements de Rouen*, I., 441.

is very scanty;[1] and opinions advanced regarding the policy
pursued by Louis VI. and even Louis VII. must necessarily be
hardly more than inferences; although with the latter there is
some degree of consistency in municipal organizations,[2] Louis
VI. really had no policy towards them save that of expediency.[3]
He favored them when it paid him so to do; he crushed them
as readily when it profited him. M. Luchaire[4] has happily
characterized his attitude as one of demi-hostility. But he was
far from allowing the movement to take its own course. The
act relating to Saint-Riquier[5] is proof positive. In the immediate realm Louis VI. was unwilling to sanction in others rights
and prerogatives rivalling his own. But from the planting of
communes in vassal territory the king received both negative and
positive benefit; negative because an obnoxious local authority
was somewhat neutralized; positive because the acquisition of local
self-government was purchased of the king with little sacrifice
of his own sovereignty.[6] The territory of the communes, further-
more, became king's land. In the eleven cases in which Louis
VI. granted communal charters, every grant is made outside of
the royal domain, save that of Dreux.[7] These were Noyon,[8]
Mantes,[9] Laon,[10] Amiens,[11] Corbie,[12] Saint-Riquier,[13] Soissons,[14]
Bruyères-sous-Laon and its dependencies, *i. e.*, Cheret, Vorges
and Valbon;[15] Beauvais,[16] Dreux,[17] and the collective commune

---

[1] Giry, *Établissements de Rouen*, I., 145.

[2] Luchaire, *Inst. Mon.*, II., 140.

[3] "Ob und inwieweit Ludwig die bereits langer bestehende Bewegung zur
Bildung sogenannter 'Kommunen' nach bestimmten Gesichtspunkten zur
Erweiterung seines Machtbereiches oder Verstärkung seines Einflusses im
Reiche auszunützen sich bemüht hat, können wir nicht nachweisen; gegen
eine solche Tendenz sprechen wenigstens die vielen Widersprüche in seinem
Verhalten gegenüber den Kommunen." — Hirsch, 13.

[4] *Les Communes Françaises*, 276.

[5] Luchaire, *Annales*, No. 372.   Guizot, *Hist. Civilization in France*.   Course
IV., Lect. 19.

[6] Walker, 104.   [7] Luchaire, *Les Communes Françaises*, 267.

[8] Luchaire, *Annales*, No. 64.   [9] *Ibid.*, No. 105.

[10] *Ibid.*, No. 124.   [13] *Ibid.*, No. 372.   [16] *Ibid.*, No. 603.

[11] *Ibid.*, No. 169.   [14] *Ibid.*, No. 377.   [17] *Ibid.*, No. 624.

[12] *Ibid.*, No. 337.   [15] *Ibid.*, No. 435.

of Vailli, Condé, Chavonnes, Celles, Pargni and Filiain, near Soissons.[1] We are in complete darkness as to the circumstances attending the foundation of Dreux; the date is unknown, even approximately (1108–1137).[2] It is probable that since the Vexin was a marcher county, Louis VI. was led to believe that a large degree of autonomy might make the place a better bulwark against the English foe. We know Philip Augustus adopted this plan with success, the suggestion of which not unlikely lay in Dreux of the Vexin.[3]

A study of the charters of the communes is instructive. Louis VI. was a soldier. As such he most needed men and money. In establishing a commune in the sphere of a feudal lord he secured the double advantage of securing money and sowing dragons' teeth in the path of the lord. The cases in which the men of a commune are granted exemption from military service are very rare.[4] In enumerating privileges granted by Louis VI. the repetition of the denial of exemption from military service is striking.[5] And yet there is little foundation for the favorite belief of historians[6] that Louis VI., in his wars, made large use of the men of the communes *as such*. Contemporary chronicles show little indication of such a host. The most of his expeditions were made at the

---

[1] Luchaire, *Annales,* No. 626. On these rural or federative communes see Luchaire, *Les Communes Françaises,* 68–96. The radiant character they had served to accentuate the movement against bishop and baron. — Luchaire, *Inst. Mon.,*II., 178.

[2] All that is known of the history of Dreux is comprehended in Luchaire, *Inst. Mon.,* II., 6, note 1.

[3] Walker, 105. "La commune était avant tout, à ses yeux, une forteresse, une instrument de guerre destiné à la defensive." — Luchaire *Les Milices communales, Acad. des Sciences moral. et polit.* 1888, p. 165.

[4] *Revue Hist.* xliv., (1890) p. 326. Prou : *De la nature du service militaire du par les roturiers aux XI*[e] *et XII*[e] *siècles.*

[5] Luchaire, *Inst. Mon.,* II., 194. *Cf.* The prohibition upon the enfranchised serfs of Laon ; see this dissertation, p. 76. n. 3. In the renunciation of rights over the lands of Saint-Martin-des-Champs in Pontoise (1128) the charter provides, "excepta sola expeditione." — Luchaire, *Inst. Mon.,* II., 150, n. 3. *Cf. Annales,* Nos. 111 (where even the bourgeois of Paris are held to service), 124, 419, 440. Boutaric 203. The customs of Lorris were exceptional in that military service was required for a day at a time only (Art. 3).

[6] Even Vuitry, I., 376 has fallen into this error.

head of the body of knights who were always around him.[1]   For a distant campaign he convoked the contingents due him, in virtue of feudal law, of seigneurs, bishops, abbots, and vassals of the crown.[2]   The church furnished contingents from the parishes, organized by their curés, as a consequence of the Truce of God, promulgated at Clermont, but such service was gratuitous and not to be confounded with the feudal service.[3]   The communes, as such, do not appear under arms, even in the army of 1124, when the emperor Henry V. thought to revive the days of the Ottos.   The terms employed by Suger indicate that forces were there from Rheims, Châlons, Laon, Soisson, Étampes, Amiens, Orléans, Paris, and the country surrounding each ; but they were there as men of a common host, not as communal troops.[4]   There is no reason to believe this host was anything else than a general *levée*, similar to that called out after the bitter defeat of Bremule,[5] (1119).   French history was not without such precedents in that time.[6]   Troops from Soissons, Amiens, Noyon, Mantes and Corbeil may have been there, though the chronicle does not say so of the last three, but they were there, not as autonomous forces, but as parts of a common army.   The revolution of the ninth century

---

[1] Even in the battle of Bremule (1119) Louis had only the knights of Paris and the Vexin. (Ord. Vit., IV., 357.)

[2] Luchaire, *Les Milices Communales, Acad. des Sciences moral. et polit.*, 1888, p. 160.   See Suger's enumeration of the vassals of the crown who went into Auvergne with Louis VI.—Suger, 108.

[3] "Où l'Église rendit un service gracieux au roi, ce fut quand elle organisa les milices paroissiales, je veux dire ces petites troupes qui, sous la conduite des curés, allaient aider le souverain à châtier les rebelles et à maintenir la paix. Mais il faut se garder de confondre le service militarie que l'Église demandait ainsi aux fidéles avec le service d'ost et de chevauchée.   Les milices dont parle Ord. Vit. etaient (Book VIII., chap. xxiv; Book XI., chap. xxxiv.; Book XII., chap. 19) une consequence immediate de la Paix de Dieu."—*Revue Hist.*, xliv., (1890) pp. 325-6.   Prou : *De la nature du service militaire du par les roturieurs aux XIe et XIIe siècles.*   For a case of a fighting priest with his parochial force, see Suger, 65.

[4] Luchaire, *Les Milices communales, Acad. des Sciences moral. et polit.*, 1888, p. 161.   See Suger's account of the projected invasion, c. xxvii.

[5] Suger, 92 ; Ord. Vit., IV., 365 ff.

[6] Luchaire, *Inst. Mon.*, II., 48-9, gives the cases.

had thrust the relations of a vassal into those of a subject and a citizen,[1] and the feudal military tenures had superseded the earlier system of public defense.[2] Louis VI., by making the bourgeois liable to bear arms, was in reality reasserting a national, and hence an old principle—a revival of the ancient duty of freemen.[3] He sought to make every man a patriot. The commune was an instrument of war to be used when the state had to fall back of its regular fighting force upon the hearths of its people, as in the case of the invasion of Henry V.[4]

Though the king obtained in the use of communal militia a body of troops which could be more promptly put in the field, when he wished, than those amenable to an intermediate noble,[5] still the chief advantage to the crown was not in the men, but in the money the communes secured to the king. The desire for money will often explain the vacillating attitude of Louis VI., and even of Louis VII. Louis VI. loved gold[6] to the verge even

[1] Baluze, t. II., 44.

[2] The inadequacy of feudal military service is well shown in the expedition which Louis directed against Thomas de Marle, when the chevaliers refused almost unanimously to cooperate with the king in the seige of Créci :—De militibus autem vix quispiam coarmari voluit, cumque aperte eis proditionis arcesseret, accitis pedestribus, ipsi, etc. (H. F., XII., 262.) Whence it appears that Louis had to rely upon contingents from ecclesiastical seigneuries. (Consult Luchaire, *Inst. Mon.*, II., 52, note 2.)

[3] See the article by M. Prou before referred to. M. Prou argues that *hostis* and *expeditio* originally had reference to any sort of military service ; that their obligation was not upon feudal tenants as such, but was a continuation of the ancient duty of freemen. I doubt if the continuity of such requirements was perfect as he holds. It seems to me that the act of Louis VI. was, as stated above, a revival of the former practice.

[4] This appears in the charter to Augere-Regis (1119). "Neque ipsi in expedicionem vel in equitatum, nisi per communitatem, scilicet si omnes communiter ire juberentur et irent."—*Ordonnances*, VII., 444. Luchaire, *Annales*, No. 273. And in this, to the serfs of the Laonnais (1129). "Masculi vero . . . . expediciones nostras bannales debent, si submoniti fiunt."—*Ibid.* p. 338.

[5] See Boutaric, 156–60.

[6] See the complaint (1120) of the people of Compiégne on account of the degradation of the coin (Luchaire, *Annales*, No. 296). Louis VI.'s act of rectification is in Mabillon, 598. Compare Luchaire, *Inst. Mon.*, I, 100 ; *Manuel*, 591. Vuitry, I., 437, cites similar complaints in 1112 and 1113.

of compromising his honor to obtain it. Amiens,[1] Laon[2] and Bruyères-sous-Laon[3] were each founded in consideration of a sum of money. The history of Laon especially, is eloquent testimony of Louis VI.'s cold-blooded way of raising money.

If the attitude of the king was determined by circumstances, that of the clergy and nobles was no less so determined; only in their case it was one of unfailing hostility.[4] The dignitaries of the church were often merely barons covered with the alb, and saw in the new institution a partial subversion of their rights [5] The words of Guibert de Nogent[6] are echoed by Bernard of Clairvaux and Ives of Chartres.[7] More than one pope demanded the abolition of a commune founded in ecclesiastical holdings.[8]

[1] At Amiens the burghers by outbidding the bishop retained their liberties. (Guib. de Nogent, X., 45) See Thierry, *Hist. du tiers-état*, 318.

[2] In the case of Laon, Louis VI granted (1111) the charter to the citizens, and then revoked it (1112) in payment of a higher sum by Gaudri, the bishop. In 1128 a charter was definitively granted. "Il est très précieux pour l'histoire du droit pénal." Violett, *Hist. du Droit français*, 115. The history of Laon has often been recounted. See Thierry, *Lettres sur l'hist. de France*, XVI.; Martin, III., 251-2; Clamageran, I., 232 ff.; Guizot, *Hist. Civilization in France*, IV., Lect. 17; Luchaire, *Annales*, Nos. 124, 132, 189, 425; Guib. de Nogent, H. F. XII., 250.

[3] Luchaire, *Inst. Mon.*, II., 175. Louis VII. was bribed to abolish Auxerre in 1175 (*Ibid.*, 176). In general, on this phase, see *Ibid.*, pp. 192-4.

[4] Luchaire, *Inst. Mon.*, II., 176; *Les Communes Françaises*, 244.

[5] Hegel surely is in error when he ascribes grants of charters by the clergy to their good will. From first to last they manifested hostility. See Luchaire, *Inst. Mon.*, II., 163. Noyon seems to afford the rare instance of a commune founded on petition of a bishop in order to reconcile the townsmen and the chapter; but this is not beyond peradventure.—See Luchaire, *Inst. Mon.*, II., 177, note 2. In Corbie the three orders united in an application to Louis le Gros.—*Ibid.*, II., 178, note 3; *Annales*, No. 337.

[6] Communis novum ac pessissimum nomen, sic se habet, ut capite censi solitum servitutis debitum dominis semel in anno solvant, etc.—*De vita sua*, Bk. III., c. vii.; H. F., XII., 250.

[7] Pacta enim et constitutiones vel etiam juramenta quae sunt contra leges canonicas vel auctoritates sanctorum Patrum, sicut vos ipsi bene nostris nullius sunt nomenti.—Epist. 77, H. F., XV., 105.

[8] For example, Pope Eugenius II. demanded the destruction of the charter of Sens (1147 or 1149) (Thierry, *Lettres sur l'Histoire de France*, XIX.), and Innocent, II., that of Rheims (*Ibid.*, XX.).

The attitude of the chatelains was hardly less tolerant. Their conduct toward the bourgeois depended largely upon their relations with the bishop. The charter of Amiens was directed against the house of Boves, which had become hereditarily invested in the chatellany,[1] while Beauvais[2] had its origin in an effort of Louis VI. to preserve the chatelain and bourgeois from the bishop.

The amount of political freedom accorded by Louis VI. varied with circumstances. In the interests of local self-government something of royal supervision had to be sacrificed; but there is little preciseness in this regard.[3] Owing to abuses by the prévôt, the commune was allowed the privilege of trying its own cases; this privilege was a conditional one, however, dependent upon strict support of law. In event of malfeasance, the rights accorded reverted to the king.[4] The process of Joslin, the bishop of Soissons, against the commune (1136) and the sentence of the court, is evidence that Louis VI. kept the communes well in hand, allowing them neither to be derelict nor arrogant.[5] In cities holding directly of the crown, there was absolute repression of the communes. The two most important cities of the realm were

---

[1] Luchaire, *Inst. Mon.*, II., 177, note 3; Thierry, *Hist. du tiers-etat*, 318 The chatelains by the twelfth century had become hereditary (see Galbert de Bruges, pp. 97, note 1 and 150, note 1, with references there given). Enguerrand de Boves was the father Thomas de Marle (Suger, 83, note 3).

[2] Luchaire, *Inst. Mon.*, II., 177, note 4. On Beauvais, see Guizot, *Hist. of Civilization in France*, IV., appendix iv. The gradual evolution of the commune of Beauvais is seen in the successive concessions of Louis VI. (Luchaire, *Annales*, Nos. 174, 198, 322, 603).

[3] Luchaire, *Inst. Mon.*, II., 191-2.

[4] *Ordonnances*, XI., Introd. xliii., by Bréquigny. *Cf.* Pardessus, 347:—"Sans doute, dans un certain nombre de communes, les habitants obtinrent le droit de choisir des magistrats, qui veillaient à l'administration intérieure, à l'exécution des statuts, à la defense générale, et qui rendaient la justice; mais c'étaient simplement des garanties pour le maintien des concessions obtenues. . . . A l'instant où les parties se trouvaient en présence, soit pour prévenir, soit pour pacifier une insurrection, le seigneur était en possession de droits, dont on ne contestait pas l'existence, et dont seulement on voulait faire réformer l'abuse ou l'extension injuste."

[5] Luchaire, *Annales*, No. 567. The process of the court is given in full in Langlois, *Textes relatifs à l'Histoire du Parlement de Paris*, No. VIII.

not communes—Paris and Orléans.[1] The privileged towns,[2] having no local independent government were favored by the king, who in the possession of privileges and exemptions made little distinction between them and the great communes. Yet Paris,[3] Orleans,[4] Étampes,[5] Bourges[6] and Compiègne[7] were better off for the restraint of the royal hand. The civil and commercial advantages which Louis VI. gave them were assured more peaceable enjoyment and more normal development, because the directive influence of the monarchy prevented such excesses as occurred at Laon or Amiens.[8]

Although no exact status can be ascribed to the communes of the reign of Louis, although they were still involved in the meshes of feudalism, yet the importance of his reign in its influence upon the communes, to the future power of the crown was very great.[9] The Tiers-État was yet in the gristle; but by

[1] Brussel, I., 182.

[2] The admirable account of these privileged towns by M. Luchaire (*Inst. Mon.*, II., 144–157) precludes any extended discussion here.

[3] Luchaire, *Annales*, Nos. 111, 303, 533, 596, 623. These acts show thas the bourgeois of Paris were the object of Louis VI.'s special solicitude. It it significant that the term *bourgeois* first occurs in his reign. The word *Burgenses* is found six times in an *ordonnance* of the year 1134. Brussel, II., 941 : Ego Ludovicus . . . . notum fieri volumus . . . . quod Burgensibus nostris Parisiensibus universis praecipimus et concedimus, etc.—Brussel, II., 941.

[4] Luchaire, *Annales*, No. 582.

[5] *Ibid.*, No. 533. This was granted in 1123, and revoked for cause in 1129. (No. 437).

[6] *Ibid.*, No. 578.

[7] *Ibid.*, No. 297.

[8] Levasseur, I., p. 186.

[9] "In France the kings used the people against the nobles as long as it suited their purpose and in the end brought nobles, people and clergy into one common bondage. This strengthening of the power of the French king within his own dominions was naturally accompanied by increased vigor in the relations of the crown to the princes who owed it a nominal homage. The reign of Louis the Fat may be set down as the beginning of that gradual growth of the Parisian monarchy which in the end swallowed up all the states which owed it homage, besides so large a part of the German and Burgundian kingdoms."—Freeman, *Norman Conquest*, V., 179. The modest beginnings of the grand vassals with respect to the communes, precluded any exercise of the king's authority save that of confirmation. In 1127 Louis VI. countersigned

an early appropriation of the commune as an instrument of crown power, Louis assured to the monarchy the bone and sinew of succeeding centuries. In after years it was largely to the cities that France was indebted for the extension of her territory. Her geographic changes were greatly modified by the revolutions of the twelfth and thirteenth centuries.[1]

the charters of St. Omer and Bruges, in Flanders (Luchaire, *Annales*, No. 384) but such intervention in the domain of a grand vassal is entirely explained by his support of William Clito (*Ibid.*, *Introd.*, cxciii.).

[1] Pigeonneau, I., 177.

CHAPTER VIII.

FOREIGN POLICY AND POLITICS.

Foreign relations occupy a place of comparatively slight importance in the reign of Louis VI., when the crown was strengthening itself intensively. England, Germany and the Papacy were
the three powers most in contact with France at this time,
but the relations with each were quite different. With England
the relations of France were political, and the point of contact,
through Normandy, was direct. With the empire and the pope
her relations were dynastic and ecclesiastical, and less vitally
connected.

The hostile attitude of England, when the French crown was
fortifying itself intensively, was most to be feared. Henry I.
had no such imperial pretensions as Rufus had entertained. His
wars were wars, not of annihilation, as his brother's had been,
but of limitation,[1] and in the fact that his schemes were so feasible
lay the danger to France. The question of the Norman-French
frontiers, therefore, becomes of greater significance than the
fighting on the borders would at first betoken.[2] As the sphere
of his activity enlarged Louis came in contact with a coalition
directed by the English king, who was aided from the first by
the powerful house of Blois[3] and later enlisted the services of
his imperial son-in-law, Henry V. of Germany, in his behalf.[4]

The wars between the two monarchs dragged on, with inter-
ruptions, over a series of years, and were waged with varying
success; but throughout, Louis VI. never lost sight of the idea

[1] Freeman, *Norman Conquest*, V., 204-5.
[2] "Verum quia Normanorum marchia, tam regum Anglorum quam Normanorum ducum nobili providentia et novorum positione castroum et invadalium flu-
minum decursu extra alias cingebatur, rex," etc.—Suger, 86. *Cf.* 6.
[3] Suger, 66.
[4] *Ibid.*, 101-3.

that the king of England was his vassal. Henry I. chafed under the rigid enforcement of a feudal right by one whom he deemed his political inferior[1] especially since his father from the day of the Conquest had disregarded the bond, and even Rufus had regarded Normandy as a land to be fought for.[2]

The pretext of the first war (1111–1113) was a dispute over the border fortress of Gisors,[3] and the enmity engendered between Louis VI. and Thibaud of Blois over the erection of a castle.[4] But back of all was the never-ending grudge between the duke of Normandy and the king of France. There were military operations in Brie in the summer of 1111, during the course of which Robert II., count of Flanders, whom Louis had summoned to his aid, was killed by a fall from his horse near the bridge of Meaux.[5] In the spring and summer of the next year the war was renewed with more intensity. Thibaud during the winter had succeeded in forming a feudal coalition against the French king, comprising Lancelin de Bulles, seigneur of Dammartin, Paien de Montjai, Ralph of Beaugerci, Milon de Brai, viscount of Troyes, the notorious Hugh de Creci, lord of Chateaufort, Guy II. of Rochefort, and Hugh, count of Troyes. The king had planned a trip to Flanders, but was apprised of the danger, while at Corbeil, by Suger, then episcopal prevot of Touri. Near Touri the royal arms were defeated by the allies, aided by the arrival of some Norman knights. Nothing daunted, however, Louis at once retrieved his fortunes. Taking advantage of the separation of his enemies, he shut up Hugh in le Puiset by fortifying Janville, over against it, and then, sustained

[1] Et quoniam "omnis potestas impatiens consortis erit" rex Francorum Ludovicus, ea qua supereminebat regi Anglorum ducique Normanorum Henrico sublimitate, in eum semper tanquam in feodatum suum efferebatur.—Suger, 85.

[2] Freeman, *Norman Conquest*, V., 193.

[3] Suger, 48.

[4] Comes Theobaldus . . . . machinebatur marchiam suam amplificare castrum erigendo in potestate Puteoli quod de feodo regis fuerat . . . . subverso igitur omino prefato castra. . . . . Theobaldus comes, fretus avunculi sui regis Anglici incliti Henrici auxilio, regi Ludovico cum complicibus suis guerram movet."—*Ibid.*, 66.

[5] Luchaire, *Annales*, No 121.

by Ralph of Vermandois and Dreu de Mouchi, he fell upon Thibaud, who was glad to fall back upon Chartres. Hugh and his chatelain then surrendered to the French king who declared Hugh deprived of his hereditary rights, and for the second time destroyed the castle of le Puiset.[1]   In the fall (1112) hostilities began again. Louis was aided by the count of Anjou and some Norman barons, among whom were Amauri de Montfort, count of Evreux, William Crispin and Robert of Bellême, the last of whom Louis sent as ambassador to the English king. But Henry thrust him into prison in Cherbourg, and in the following year he was carried over to England.[2]   The winter of 1112–3 cooled the ardor of the combatants. In March the two kings held a conference near Gisors, and there peace was made. Louis renounced in favor of Henry the suzerainty of the seigneury of Bellême as well as his claims upon the counties of Maine and Brittany. The French barons who had taken part against their lord gained nothing by their espousal of Henry's cause, for the English king let them lie at the mercy of their overlord.[3]

In the interval of peace Henry I. tried to force the Norman baronage to do homage to the Aetheling William (1115). The attempt provoked a counter-movement by Louis VI. in favor of William Clito, Henry's nephew by his brother Robert. The French king meant to give to Normandy a master who would never be seated upon the throne of England.[4]   In the absence of Henry I. from Normandy, the duty of guarding the English interests fell upon Thibaud. Louis had made an alliance with Foulque, the count of Anjou, and with Baldwin VII., the new count of Flanders. A desultory conflict was carried on throughout the summer and autumn of 1116 in the Vexin, Picardy and in the vicinity of Chartres.[5]   In the next summer, however, the French king and the count of Flanders entered Normandy.

[1] Luchaire, *Annales*, No. 134.

[2] *Ibid.*, Nos. 148, 149.

[3] *Ibid.*, No. 158.

[4] Freeman, *Norman Conquest*, V., 187.

[5] Luchaire, *Annales*, No. 207.

But the danger had been great enough to call Henry from beyond sea and the French host had to retreat before the army of Henry, composed of English, Normans and Bretons (summer of 1117).[1] During the winter the coalition formed by the French king against Henry I. was augmented by the addition of several of the Norman baronage, especially of Enguerran de Chaumont. Early in the spring of 1118 the united forces entered the Vexin, surprised the Chateau de Gasny and attacked with success the new fortress Malassis, both of which fortresses had been newly erected by the English king. It is not improbable, even, that the French forces ravaged Normandy as far as Rouen.[2]

But Louis VI. was no match for the king of the English. Even in force of arms he was surpassed by Henry I. while in diplomacy and intrigue he was far the inferior of his English rival, as the result of Henry's winter machinations proved to him. The war had been renewed as usual with the beginning of spring (1119),[3] but Henry was in no hurry to begin active hostilities. While Louis occupied himself in insignificant sieges along the Andelle and Epte rivers, the English king succeeded in estranging Louis' most powerful ally. Foulque (1109–1142) of Anjou was lured away from the side of the French king by the marriage of his daughter to the English heir, the Ætheling William,[4] thus leaving the count of Flanders the only staunch ally upon whom Louis could depend.

In August Louis crossed the Andelle river and entered Normandy. Henry was at Noyon-sur-l'Andelle. In the plain of Brémule, in spite of the efforts of Burchard of Montmorenci to dissuade the French king, the two armies met in combat (August 20, 1119). The battle of Brémule was a complete rout

[1] Luchaire, *Annales*, No. 229.

[2] *Ibid.*, No. 233. Suger, 86–9 and Ord. Vit., IV., 311, differ in details.

[3] *Ibid.*, Nos. 252, 257, 258.

[4] Comes etiam Andegavensis Fulco, cum et proprio hominio et multis sacramentis, obsidum etiam multiplicate regi Ludovico confederatus esset, avaritiam fidelitate preponens, inconsulto rege, perfidia infamatus, filiam suam regis Anglici filio Guilelmo nuptui tradidit.—Suger, 91. See Freeman, *Norman Conquest*, V., 184.

of the French forces.[1]   In bitter shame Louis returned to Paris, where Amauri de Montfort revived his courage by advising a general muster of contingents under bishops, counts and other lords.   The fyrd gathered from near and far.   Forces came from Bourgogne, Berry and Auvergne in the south, from Lille, Tournai and Arras in Flanders, as well as from the nearer localities of Senonais, Laonnais, Beauvaisis, Vermandois, Étampes and Noyon.[2] The new host invaded Normandy, burned Ivri and began the siege of Breteuil.[3]   Ralph the Breton, however, succeeded in holding the place until the arrival of Henry I.   The French king then turned his arms against the count of Blois.   Owing, however, to the intercession of the chapter of Notre-Dame de Chartres, and the bourgeois, Chartres was spared from flames,[4] and Louis dispersed his troops in order to meet Pope Calixtus II.

The advantage Louis now took of the presence of Calixtus in France is probably the least commendable event of his reign. Nothing short of a moral preponderance could remove the sting of defeat from the breast of the French king.   In the council of Rheims (October 20–30, 1119), the king set forth in detail his complaint against Henry, appearing in person before that august body.   He told how Henry I. had seized upon his fief of Normandy and deprived its lawful duke of his heritage; how Henry had imprisoned his own nephew, William the Clito, and his ambassador, Robert of Bellême, and had stirred up Count Thibaud, his

---

[1] In quo bello fugit ipse rex Ludovicus, captique sunt ibi pene omnes Franciae proceres et optimates.—*Ex chron. mortui-maris*, H. F., XII., 782.   The territorial idea in the word "Franciae" is to be observed.   Suger (90–1) disguises the true nature of this battle.   *Cf.* Ord. Vit., IV., 355–363 and Luchaire, *Annales*, Nos. 257, 258, 259, 260, 261, 262.   Freeman (*Norman Conquest*, V., 186–190), and Norgate (I., 235–7) have each a good account.   Velly relates that in the battle of Brémule an English knight having seized the bridle of Louis' horse, cried out, "The king is taken!"   Louis, as he felled the boaster, rejoined, "Do you not know that in the game of chess the king is never taken?"—an indication of his spirit if not his good judgment on that occasion.—(*Hist. de France*, II., 14.   But no authorities are cited.)

Ord. Vit., IV., 364–5; 366–9; Suger, 92.

[3] *Ibid.; Chron. Maurin*, H. F., XII., 74.

[4] *Ibid.*

vassal. The French prelates vouched for the truth of their king's accusations. The feeling of the assembly ran so high that Geoffrey, the archbishop of Rouen, who rose to vindicate his lord, was forced to desist. But Calixtus was not to be duped; he would be arbiter, but not a cat's-paw. Accordingly he tried to satisfy Louis by hurling an anathema at the English king's imperial son-in-law Henry V. a proceeding which satisfied the pope far more than the French king, and then employed himself in making terms between the two monarchs.[1] Calixtus met Henry in a conference at Gisors (22–27 Nov.). As a result, within a year, all castles and prisoners taken by either side were restored, and Louis VI. agreed to abandon the cause of the Pretender, Clito, in return for which concession, Henry's son, the Aetheling, by the father's command, *again* did homage to the king of France, his overlord. This fact of homage is remarkable, as there is no record of any homage done by either William Rufus or Henry.[2]

Within a year the loss of the English heir in the *White Ship* (1120) was destined to precipitate hostilities once more. On the failure of the English male line, Louis saw an opportunity more favorable than before, of giving to Normandy a duke who would

---

[1] For the details of the Council of Rheims, see Luchaire, *Annales*, No. 266. Ord. Vit., IV., 372–393, and Guil. de Nangis, 10 (*Société de l'Hist. de France*). Suger, 94, differs in his account of Louis VI. from Ord Vit. The text follows the latter. Freeman (*Norman Conquest*, V., 190–2) has a vivid account. The importance of the council of Rheims lies in the fact *the pope has become the court of last resort for kings.*

[2] Freeman, *Norman Conquest*, V. 193. For details see Ord. Vit., IV., 398–406. Luchaire, *Annales*, Nos. 267, 298. Freeman has missed the fact that Henry I.'s son did homage to Louis VI. at the end of the first war. "Cum autem Guilelmus regis anglici filius, regi Ludovico hominium suum fecisset," etc. —Suger, 52. The homage of Henry I.'s son is found in Will. Malms. V. 405:— Ordinibat (Henricus) . . . . ut hominium quod ipse pro culmine imperii fastideret facere, filius delicatus et qui putabatur viam sæculi ingressurus non recusaret. A fuller account is in H. F., XIV., 16. *Ex Anonymi Blandinensis appendicula ad Sigbertum:*—Ludovicus rex Francorum contra regem Angliæ vadit, et usque Rotomagum omnia vastat, tandem conventum fuit ut Willelmus filius Henrici Regis Anglorum Normanniam teneret de rege Franciæ, et hommagium sibi faceret, sicut Rollo primus Normanniæ Dux jure perpetuo promiserat.

never be king of England.[1] He had a ready ally in Foulque, who
had returned from Jerusalem and demanded the dowry of his
daughter, the widow of the ill-starred Aetheling. But Henry I.
was able to stir up a formidable adversary against the French
king, and for the first time since the days of the Ottos, France
and the Empire came into actual contact. England and the
Empire had a common bond in that Henry V., the emperor,
had married Matilda, daughter of the English king. It was
Henry V., the German emperor, whom Henry I. now stirred
up against his foe.[2] The war which hitherto had been of
feudal character, now becomes a triangular conflict of international importance.[3] The new adversary was enough to tax the
prowess of a greater king than Louis VI. The most intense form
of common interest is common danger, and the greatest danger
of a people has always been war. The unanimity with which the
vassals responded to the king's call, and the extent of the summons, indicates a fervor approaching a national manifestation.
There is evidence of latent nationality in the fact that barons
who resisted the crown and struggled for petty independence at
home, now, when exterior danger threatened, stood by the king
in common cause.[4] The muster roll[5] included all in the immediate realm, a *levée en masse*, besides the feudal contingents of the

[1] Although the participation of Louis VI., in the plans of William Clito and
Foulque of Anjou is not formally indicated, there is no doubt that he favored
them. See Luchaire, *Annales*, No. 334.

[2] England appears upon the general scene of European politics as the
enemy of France and the ally of Germany. . . . . When the two Henrys are
joined together against the Parisian king, we have the very state of things
which Europe has since seen so many times repeated, from the day of English
overthrow at Bouvines to the day of victory at Waterloo.—Freeman, *Norman
Conquest*, V., 197.

[3] We now get evidence of a *national antagonism* between the two realms.
Thus Ekkehard (*Mon. Germ. Hist.*, VI., 262) says—"Teutonici non facile
gentes impugnant exteras." And Suger (102) puts these words in the mouth of
Louis VI. : "Transeamus audacter ad eos, ne redeuntes impune ferant, quod
in terrarum dominam Franciam superbe presumpserunt," *Cf.* p. 30, where he
speaks of "furor Theutonicus."

[4] Luchaire, *Inst. Mon.*, II., 274 ; Daniel, I., 357.

[5] "Rex . . . . ut eum tota Francia sequatur potenter invitat."—Suger. 102.
Suger's numbers, though, certainly are exaggerated. See Vuitry, I., 376, note.

Duke of Bourgogne, William VII, Duke of Aquitaine, and the Counts of Flanders, Champagne, Vermandois. Conan III. of Brittany, Charles the Good of Flanders, and Count Foulque, were late in coming, however, "because the length of the road and the brief time prevented."[1] The immediate object of the imperial attack was Rheims,[2] whence the papal anathema had been launched, but ere the imperial army had gone further than Champagne, the emperor had to return,[3] and the death in the next year of the last emperor of the Franconian house, removed all danger from the East. Meanwhile the Norman rebels had been crushed by Henry I. at Bourgtheroulde, and the silken oriflamme which Louis VI. had snatched from the altar of St. Denis,[4] destined

[1] See Suger's account, pp. 103-4. Of the last three he says "quod . . . . vie prolixitas et temporis brevitas prohiberet." A manuscript in the Bibliothéque nationale, recently published by M. Paul Viollet (*Une grand chronique de Saint Denis. Observations pour servir à l'histoire critique des Oeuvres de Suger, Bib. de l'École des Chartes*, xxxiv., 1873, p. 244) interestingly shows how opinion was divided as to the manner of meeting the imperial army :— "Inquit (Louis VI.) quid inde agendum esset. Ibi dum varie varii opinarentur et aliqui hostes dignum ducerent præstotari, dicentes eos in regni medio facilius expugnandos, alii villas regni murari, et oppida pugilibus muniri dignum ducerent, rex Teutonicam rapacitatem abhorrens, et damnum irreparabile si permitterentur ingredi spatiumque deesset muniendi civitates et oppida : "Non sic," inquit, "sed delectum militum sine mora colligendum censeo et in extremo termino regni nostro loco mari validissimi adversarios expectare pede fixo." On this levy see Boutaric, 255 ff. On the participation of the Duke of Bourgogne, see Ernest Petit, *Hist. des Ducs de Bourgogne*, I., 337-8. Inasmuch as the Count of Flanders was vassal of the emperor, also, it is not unreasonable to believe the "delay" of Charles was premeditated.

[2] Suger, 101 ; *Annal. S. Bened.*, VI., 113.

[3] The reason for this sudden retreat is involved in obscurity. The most probable cause is that of a popular uprising in Worms. (Ekkehard, *Mon Germ. Hist., SS.*, VI., 262-3.) Suger (105-6) is too gleeful to be reliable. On the election of Lothar of Saxony and its effect on France, see this dissertation, p. 53.

[4] Suger, 102 ; Tardif, No. 391. The oriflamme was a red silk banner, three-pointed, tipped with green and hung upon a gilt spear. Originally the banner of the Count of the Vexin (Tardif, No. 391), when that county fell to the king (1107) the oriflamme became the national ensign. See DuCange, *Dissert.*, XVII., *Oeuvres de Suger (Soc. de l'Hist. de France)*, 442-3. Daniel, I. 358. An ancient description of the oriflamme is in *Guillaume le Breton*, Book XI., 32-9.

from that day forth to be the national banner of France, drooped on its standard.[1]

In the next few years the widowed empress married Geoffrey, son of Foulque the Black of Anjou, (1128) and the luckless Clito was consoled with the hand of Adeliza, half-sister of Louis' queen, and a grant of the French Vexin (1127).[2]

But peace again was of short duration. This time, however, the war was not of Louis' choosing ; Henry I. was the aggressor. The occasion was one of the accidents of history,— the murder of Charles the Good of Flanders.   Probably no single event from the capture of Jerusalem to the fall of Edessa so startled Europe as the murder of the Count of Flanders on the very steps of the altar of the church of St. Donatien, in Bruges (March 2, 1127).

From the beginning of the twelfth century, the counts of Flanders had been on good terms with their French suzerain.[3] In the wars with Henry I., Baldwin VII. had sustained the crown of France until his death, in 1119.[4]   He left his title to his nephew Charles, surnamed the Good.[5]   Charles held to a neutral course in the wars between the kings of France and England, though he did not fail in loyalty to Louis le Gros.[6]   The good reputation of Charles soon won him the respect of Europe. In 1123 he declined an offer of the crown of Jerusalem, because

It was at this time that Louis VI. enunciated the principle that the king could do homage to none.   See this dissertation, p. 44.

[1] On the third war between Louis VI. and Henry I., see *Norman Conquest,* V., 196–9.

[2] Luchaire, *Annales,* No. 378.

[3] For the early relations of Flanders and France, see Pfister, *Le Règne de Robert le Pieux,* 218–224.

[4] Ord. Vit.. IV., 316 ; Herman de Tournai, *Mon. Germ. Hist.* SS. XIV., 284.

[5] Galbert de Bruges, 3, and notes 1 and 3.   Galbert calls him (p. 9) "Catholicus, bonus, religiosus, cultor Dei hominumque rector providus."   See his eulogy, 6.   Charles the Good was son of Canute IV. of Denmark and of Adela, daughter of the former Count of Flanders, Robert the Frison.   Baldwin VII. was a grandson of the last and succeeded his father, Robert I., in 1111. Charles was also cousin of Louis VI. by marriage.—Galbert de Bruges, 75, note 7.

[6] William Malms., III., 257.   He was in the army against Henry V. and also took part in the expedition into Auvergne.—Suger, 103, 108.

he would not desert his fatherland;[1] and two years afterwards the princes of the Empire offered him, in vain, the imperial scepter.[2]

On March 2, 1127, the Count of Flanders was murdered at the instigation of Bertulf, the prevot of Bruges, because the count had discovered, in a judicial duel, his servile origin, which wealth and power had hitherto obscured. The news of the murder ran like wildfire though Europe.[3] Flanders was in a tumult. For seven days riot raged through the streets of Bruges. There were traitors among the people; neither life nor property was safe. At last the dead count's chamberlain, Gervais, succeeded in organ-

[1] Galbert de Bruges, c. 5.

[2] *Ibid.*, c. 4. But see Giesebrecht, IV., 417, who thinks the movement not so spontaneous as Galbert's account indicates. *Cf.* Otto of Friesing, VII., 17.

[3] This is no exaggeration. "Cum tam gloriosi principis martirium vita suscepisset, terrarum universi habitatores infamia traditionis ipsius perculsi, nimis indoluerunt, et mirabile dictu, occiso consule in castro Brugensi, in mane unius diei, scilicet feriae quartae, fama impiae mortis ejus in Londonia civitate, quae est in Anglia terra, secundo die postea circa primam diei perculit cives, et circa vesperam ejusdem secundae diei Londunenses turbavit, qui in Francia a nobis longe remoti sunt; sicut didicimus per scholares nostros, qui eodem tempore Londuni studuerunt, sic etiam per negotiotores nostros intelleximus, qui eodem die Londoniae mercaturae intenti fuere. Intervalla ergo vel tempo rum vel locorum predictorum nec equo nec navigio quispiam transisse tam velociter poterat."—Galbert de Bruges, 22. *Cf.* Robert de Torigni, *Mon. Germ. Hist.* SS., VI., 488. An account of the judicial duel, the plot of Bertulf and his nephews, and a detailed relation of the murder of Charles the Good will be found in Galbert de Bruges, cc. 7–15.

The following note of M. Pirenne (Edition of Galbert de Bruges, 75, note 7), I quote entire; it explains itself: "On ne peut admettre avec M. Molinier (ed. de Suger, p. 111, n. 2) que Louis VI. ait été de connivance avec les assassins de Charles; sa conduite prouve précisément le contraire. D'ailleurs il est inexact que Charles fût allié au roi d'Angleterre *depuis plusieurs années déjà* en 1127. En 1126, il avait pris part avec un contingent de troups à l'expedition du roi de France en Auvergne (Suger, pp. 108–110). Il est vrai que Charles abandonna la politique systématiquement hostile de Baudoin VI. vis à vis de l'Angleterre; mais cette conduite prudente et d'accord avec les interests de la Flandre (See *Norman Conquest*, V., 187,—J. W. T.) ne peut avoir poussé Louis VI. à tremper dans le crime de Bertulf et de ses neveux. Un poeme anonyme sur la mort de Charles (De Smet, *Corp. Chron. Flander.*, I., p. 79) commence par les mots : '*Anglia ridet, Francia luget, Flandria languet.*'"

izing the popular fury. The murderers and their accomplices shut themselves up in the burgh [1] of the town (March 9, 1127.) A regular siege was now began. The men of Bruges were reinforced by those of Ghent bringing arms and instruments of siege.[2] For ten days it was prolonged. Then the court yard of the castle was forced and the imprisoned conspirators retreated to the church (March 19). Thence they were driven by the maddened populace to seek cover in the tower. The sacred character of the edifice did not protect it. Not a shred of the interior furniture remained. In the meanwhile Louis VI. had arrived at Arras,[3] (March 8, about) whence he sent greeting to the princes and barons of the siege, assuring them that he would come as soon as a new count was elected.[4] This was imperative, not only for the peace of Flanders, but in order to avoid complications of a graver sort. The chief competitors were Thierry of Elsass[5] and William of Normandy,[6] the Clito. But a swarm of other candidates arose, among whom were Thierry [7] Count of Holland, Arnold,[8] nephew of Charles the Good, and Baldwin IV.,[9] Count of Hainaut.

[1] It is indispensable to understand the topography of the burgh. It was protected by a moat over which were four bridges. The walls were nearly sixty feet high and were flanked with towers. In the interior were various structures disposed about the court. These were the church of Saint Donatien; the house of the count, which was connected by a gallery with the church; the school, the cloister, the refectory of the monks, and the house of the canonical *prevot.* See Galbert de Bruges, pp. 20, note 3; 49, note; and the map opposite p. 1.

[2] *Ibid.,* c. 40.   [3] *Ibid.,* c. 47.   [4] *Ibid.*

[5] He was cousin of Charles the Good and descended through the female line from Robert the Frison (1071–1093). See Galbert de Bruges, 3, note 3; 76, note 4, 5.

[6] The grandson of the Conqueror was a distant cousin of Charles the Good. —*Ibid.,* 82, note 2.

[7] Thierry of Holland had least to claim to the succession. See the claim, *Ibid.* 56, note 5.

[8] By Charles' sister Ingertha.—*Ibid.,* 138, note 2.

[9] Grandson of Baldwin VI. Count of Flanders (1067–1070) and brother of Count Robert the Frison, who violently deprived his nephews of their rights. In the assembly at Arras, Baldwin asserted a claim founded on these events.— *Ibid.,* 108, note 11. Freeman (*Norman Conquest,* V., 206) says that Henry I. of England was a candidate. He is surely in error.

Legitimacy pointed to Thierry of Elsass[1] or Baldwin of Hainaut.[2] Arnold was strong only in that the hearts of the bourgeois of Bruges were with him,[3] while the Count of Holland was a shallow pretender. The issue really was a contest between the king of England and Louis VI. of France for control of the election. William of Normandy was a deadly enemy of his uncle, hence Louis VI. sought to promote an anti-Anglican alliance by securing him the countship of Flanders.[4] It was no less the interest of Henry I. to foil such a move. Neither Thierry of Elsass nor Arnold could be dangerous.[5] The French king, however, had the advantage of being on the ground. In the meeting at Arras, whither Thierry of Elsass had sent his petition for election, he practically forced the election of his protégé (March 23) upon the nobles of Flanders.[6] Baldwin of Hainaut quitted the assembly in a rage, and at once formed a coalition[7] in favor of Henry I. against the French king, which comprised Stephen of Blois, the duke of Louvain, Thomas de Couci, and William of Ypres.[8]

Meanwhile William Clito's election had been ratified by the

[1] Galbert de Bruges, 108. *Cf.* Giry, *Hist. de la Ville de Saint-Omer*, I., 47 and note 2.

[2] *Ibid.*, supra.

[3] Galbert de Bruges, 108.

[4] *Ibid.*, 82, note 2; Suger, 112, note 4.

[5] Galbert de Bruges, 147, note 2. *Ibid.*, 76.

[6] See Galbert's account (c. 52) of this meeting of the "principes Franciae et primi terrae Flandriarum." The whole account is a graphic picture of feudal manners, as many another touch of Galbert's is. (*Cf.* c. 56 and Waitz, VII., 51 ff.). The French policy is clearly set forth. It is worth noticing that the territorial character of France comes out and that Louis le Gros is "Franciae imperator." See this dissertation, p. 109.

[7] Luchaire, *Annales*, No. 379, c.

[8] William of Ypres was a veritable *condottiere* of the twelfth century. He was a natural son of Philip de Loo, son of Robert the Frison. He was hated by the Flemings for his cruelty. He organized a hireling troop under the name of Brabançons, and was in the service of Henry I. After Henry's death (1135), Stephen used him to promote the anarchy of his reign, and rewarded him with the county of Kent. In 1155, Henry II. expelled him from England. He died ten years later in his native country. See Galbert de Bruges, *passim;* especially pp. 35, note 2. 55 and note 4; 57 and note 1; 146, note 3. There

burghers of Bruges (April 2),[1] and despite his unpopularity he had received the homage[2] of the dead count's vassals (April 6). The new count sought to win the good will of all. To the clergy he granted immunities; to the noblesse he abandoned the confiscated goods of the assassins and purchased the grace of the bourgeois of Bruges by a grant of privileges[3] (April 6), which Louis VI. confirmed a week later (April 14). To St. Omer he also granted a charter.[4]

In the interval the crowd, holding at bay the band in the tower of St. Donatien, had been resting on their arms. At last on April 12 the king and Count William began an attack upon the tower. The besieged retreated to the top,[5] where for six days they successfully withstood every assault. Then Louis gave orders to sap the tower (April 18). The captives who had held out for forty-one days in all, now abandoned hope; the foulness of their quarters, which were too narrow to allow all to recline at once, added to hunger and thirst, made them succumb (April 19). One by one they crawled through a window and descended by a rope.[6] But their sufferings were by no means at an end. Pending the funeral of Charles the Good,[7] which took place on April 22, they were thrust into the dungeons of the castle.[8] There they lingered in the darkness, dampness and stench for over two weeks. In the interval, Louis and Count William had been called to Ypres and thence to Oudenarde, on account of trouble

is a memoir by De Smet.—*Notice sur Guillaume d'Ypres et les Compagnies franches du Brabant et de la Flandre au Moyen-age. (Mem. Acad. Belg.,* t. XV.). On the employment of mercenary troops consult Boutaric, 240-2; *Bibliothèque de l'École de Chartes,* III., p. 123, 417; Giraud, *Les roturiers au XII*[e] *siècle. Ibid.,* 1841-2.

[1] Galbert de Bruges, c. 54. *Cf. Revue d'Histoire et d'Archeologie,* Bruxelles, 1860, p. 113 ff.

[2] *Ibid.,* c. 56. *Cf.* Waitz, VII., 51 ff. Galbert's account is the fullest presentation of this feudal ceremony extant.

See abstract in Luchaire, *Annales,* No. 382.

[4] *Ibid.,* 55. The text of the charter is in Giry, *Hist. de St. Omer,* 52 ff. Luchaire, *Annales,* 384, has an abstract of it.

[5] Galbert de Bruges, c. lxiv.

[6] See details, Galbert de Bruges, cc. 73-5; Suger, 112.

[7] *Ibid.,* c. 76.   [8] *Ibid.,* c. 74.

created by William of Ypres, who was apprehended and imprisoned in Lille. They did not return until May 4 to Bruges.[1]
Then followed an act on the part of William, and sustained by
Louis VI. which ultimately cost the count-regnant his title and
destroyed for France the balance she had secured in Flanders,
against England. The defenders of the tower were condemned
without form or process, practically by martial law, and hurled
one after another, eight and twenty in all, from the coping of
the tower which had for so long been their prison-house (May
5).[2] On the day following Louis VI. quitted Flanders for
France.

An investigation of the conspiracy against Charles and an
attempt to apprehend the parties guilty of plundering the
palace, followed this summary execution. William's conduct
was a grave political blunder. The whole affair was an assertion
of martial law, and on the lines upon which it was carried out,
was an usurpation of the jurisdiction of the local echevinage,
and alienated a class powerful by virtue of wealth, position
and long-acquired authority. Moreover, it was a direct viola-
tion of a privilege he had himself so shortly before accorded
the men of Bruges.[3] This state of feeling was aggravated
still more by an effort on his part to exact the *tonlieu* of the
burghers[4] which excited popular antagonism, culminating in
the revolt of Lille followed by other towns in Flanders, and

[1] Galbert de Bruges, cc. 78–9; Suger, 113–4.

[2] *Ibid.*, c. 81, and p. 125, note 2.

[3] *Ibid.*, cc. lxxxvii.–viii. and notes. The charter given to St. Omer (Art. I.)
recognizes this local jurisdiction; it is by inference, however, that the privilege is extended to Bruges.—*Ibid.*, p. 96, note.

[4] *Ibid.*, c. 88. "Dans l'affaire du tonlieu de Bruges, Guillaume de
Normandie devait nécessairement se prononcer en faveur de la noblesse. Ayant
avant tout besoin de soldats pour résister aux adversaires que lui suscitait la
politique anglaise, il ne pouvait mécontenter les chevaliers. Les nécessités politiques le forcèrent donc, comme un peu plus tard les empereurs de la maison de
Hohenstaufen en Allemagne, à agir contre les villes pour conserver l'appui de
la noblesse. Guillaume n'avait d'ailleurs abandonné le tonlieu aux Brugeois
que pour assurer son élection. Mais en réalité cette concession était exorbitante.
Après la mort de Guillaume, Thierry d'Alsace se garda de la renouveler."—M.
Pirenne, in Galbert de Bruges, p. 132, note 5.

the expulsion of William.[1]   The repose following his accession
had been momentary.   The misconduct of the new count and
the intrigues of the king of England, who still plotted for
Thierry of Elsass once more made Flanders the theatre of fierce
turmoil.   Thierry of Elsass reappeared in Bruges and was elected
count of Flanders by the burghers of Bruges and Ghent (March
30, 1128).[2]   Again an assembly was convoked at Arras, but the
sturdy burghers refused to go (April 10).[3]   Again Louis VI. and
the English king were at swords' points.   Once more Flanders
was torn by civil war.   The Clito returned from the siege of
Bruges (May 29).[4]   Louis was defeated under the walls of Lille
(May 21) and forced to fall back upon France which Henry I.
was invading[5] (June–July), when under the walls of Alost (July
27) death ended the career of William Clito, the man whom for-

[1] Galbert de Bruges, cc. 93–8.

[2] *Ibid.*, cc. 102.

[3] Their response is an amazing declaration of independence.   One under-
stands in reading their rejoinder whence the spirit came of the men who wres-
tled upon the dikes of Holland against the thraldom of Spain and fought in the
trenches with Maurice of Nassau: Notum igitur facimus universis, tam regi quam
ipsius principibus, simulque presentibus et successoribus nostris, quod nihil per-
tinet ad regem Franciae de electione vel positione comitis Flandriae si sine
herede aut cum herede obiisset.   Terrae compares et cives proximum comitatus
heredem eligendi habent potestatem, et in ipso comitatu sublimandi possident
libertatem.   Pro jure ergo terrarum, quas in feodum tenuerit a rege, cum
obierit consul, pro eodem feodo dabit successor comitis armaturam tantum-
modo regi.   Nihil ulterius debet consul terrae Flandriae regi Franciae, neque
rex habet rationem aliquam, ut potestative seu per coemptionem seu per pre-
tium nobis superponat consulem, aut aliquem preferat.   Sed quia rex et comites
Flandriae cognationis natura hactenus conjuncti stabant, eo respectu milites et
proceres et cives Flandriae assensum regi prebuerant de eligendo et ponendo
illo Willelmo sibi in consulem.   Sed aliud est prorsus quod ex cognatione
debetur, aliud vero quod antiqua predecessorum Flandriae consulum traditione
ac justitia examinatur instituta.—Galbert de Bruges, chap. cvi.   But consult
the editor's commentary, note.   M. Luchaire (*Inst. Mon.*, II., 24–25) says of
this that, " La royauté recevait ainsi une véritable leçon de droit féodal."   It
seems to me that it is more than this.   It implies a quasi self-consciousness,
an idea of the unity of one people of one blood under one government, and
that to be their own.

[4] *Ibid.*, c. 112.

[5] Henry of Huntingdon, p. 247.

tune had never favored.[1] Thierry of Elsass, whose popularity already had installed him in the popular heart, by the mutual consent of Henry I. and Louis VI. was invested with the title of Count of Flanders[2] and regranted[3] the concessions made by the grandson of the Conqueror.[4] It was not even a Pyrrhic victory for the French king,[5] he had been checkmated in every move by his astute English rival.[6] Only one thing was secured — the boon of peace.[7]

The territorial aggrandizement of France during the reign of Louis VI. was insignificant until his last year. He saw rightly that the extension of sovereignty depended upon the means of exercising that sovereignty;[8] therefore, with the melancholy exception of Flanders,[9] he limited his activity to the field in

---

[1] On the death of William Clito, see Galbert de Bruges, c. cxix.

[2] *Ibid.*, c. 102.

[3] *Ibid.*, c. 122.

[4] There is a good account of this episode in Giry, *Hist. de la Ville de Saint Omer*, I., c. vi.. secs. 1–4.

[5] Thierry did not do homage to Louis VI. according to Ord. Vit., XII., 45, until 1132. It is an interesting fact that the speech of the burghers of Bruges was pleaded relative to the right of suzerainty between the kings of France and the counts of Flanders as late as the time of Louis XI.—Galbert de Bruges, 176, note.

[6] Luchaire, *Annales*, Nos. *in loco*, has a detailed account of the history, so far as it pertains to Louis le Gros. See also Introd., pp. xcv–cii.

[7] *Ex chronico mauriniacensi*, H. F., XII., 72. Tunc misericordia Dei super Franciam respiciens, perfectissimam concordiam inter eos misit; et capite seditionis extincto, quietis securitas agricolarum pectora laetificavit.

[8] "Le progrès territorial s'accomplissait parallèlement au progrès politique."—Luchaire, *Inst. Mon*, II., 260.

[9] In the case of Flanders, it must be said, that there were extenuating circumstances. Louis VI. was not weak as a suzerain, nor was Henry I. strong in his own strength, with reference to Flanders. Henry's advantage lay in the fact that he espoused the candidate whom the people wanted. The moral opposition of the Flemings defeated Louis VI. more than sheer force of arms. And even in Flanders Louis VI. did not wholly depart from his policy. Hermann de Tournai (M. G. H., SS. xiv., 294) distinctly says that he cast aside for prudential reasons, the countship of Flanders either for himself or for his sons:—Et quia plures filios habebat, et uni eorum Flandriam daret, suggerebant. Sed rex, ut vir prudentissimus, considerans nullum filiorum suorum adhuc esse duo-

which it was possible for him to be efficient. Acquisition was confined to repairing, either by annexation, confiscation or subjugation, the breaches in the frontier. Besides the commune of Dreux,[1] he had strengthened the border in other places. The districts Louis redeemed from local tyrannies were attached to the territory of the crown as counties or chatellanies. Montlhery, Rochefort, Ferte-Alais and the lands of Hugh de Puiset were united to the crown as the county of Corbeil.[2] Cases like this afforded Louis VI. an invaluable opportunity to establish a local government free from the taint of tradition.[3] The Gâtinais was increased by Yèvre-le-Chatel and Chambon, bought of Foulque, and strongholds were erected at Montchauvet, Grès, Moret, le Chatellier, Janville and Charlevanne, to insure peace along the margins of the royal domain,[4] as Montlheri, Ferte-Alais, le Puiset and Chateaufort gave tranquillity to Orléannais and the region of Étampes. Such acquisitions, though acquired by means recognized by feudal law, were, however, held by royal tenure and hence tended to the homogeneity of the realm.[5] By being faithful over a little—by being faithful to the ancient patrimony of the Capetians, Louis VI. made it possible for Philip Augustus and St. Louis to be rulers over much.[6] Even

dennem nec sine magistro qui ei jugiter adhaereret, tam indomitam posse regere gentem, et ei se non posse semper esse praesentem ; timens ne aliquid exinde mali eis contingeret, altiori consilio refugit aliquem ex eis terrae proeficere.

[1] All that is known of Dreux is grouped in Luchaire, *Inst. Mon.*, II., 6, note.

[2] Il avait fallu vingt ans au pouvoir royal pour éteindre les petites tyrannies locales de Montlhery, de Rochefort, de la Ferte-Alais, du Puiset, et pour réunir à la couronne leurs possessions territoriales, aussi que le comté de Corbeil. De toutes ces seigneuries, celle de Montlhery était la plus importante et elle s'accrut encore de terres et de fiefs appartenant à des arrière-vassaux entraînés dans la révolte de leur suzerain.—Vuitry, I., 185. The prévotés of Corbeil, Montlhery, Saint Leger and Yveline, which figure in the account of 1202 are of this origin.

[3] Luchaire, *Manuel*, 265.

[4] Luchaire, *Inst. Mon.*, II., 260-1.

[5] "Le domaine royal s'agrandit au moyen de contrats propres au régime féodal, tenant moins du droit public que du droit privé," *i. e.*, the right of the king.—Vuitry, I., p. 21.

[6] "Philip reared the structure of government on foundations already laid.

as it was, so imposing was his reputation among the princes of
Europe that in the second year of his undivided rule (1109)
Raymond-Bérenger III., the Count of Barcelona, implored his
succor against the Saracens of Spain;[1] and Bohemond of
Antioch thought he was strengthened in the eyes of the Infidel
because he had married the sister of the King of France (1106).[2]
But the theory of the Middle Ages which regarded the empire as
an international power, went farther than the name of king, and
sometimes attributed to Louis VI. even the imperial title itself.[3]
Such ascription, however, was evanescent. The growing unity of
France shunned a title which implied so little nationality. In its
stead the royal prestige found expression in the title of "Most
Christian King," which, from the time of Louis le Gros, is generally attached to the princes of the Capetian house.[4]

A developer rather than an innovator, his reign brought into bloom the germs
which had come into being under Louis VI . . . . and which the chill and
feeble rule of Louis VII. could not destroy."—Walker, 144.

[1] Luchaire, *Annales*, No. 73; Petit, *Hist. des Ducs de Bourgogne*, I., 291-2;
H. F., xii., 281.

[2] "Tanta etenim et regni Francorum et domini Ludovici preconabatur
strenuitas, ut ipsi etiam Saraceni hujus terrore copule terrerentur."—Suger, 23.

[3] So Galbert de Bruges (c. 52) uses the words "secundum consilium regis
Ludewici, Franciae imperatoris" (1127). In a charter of 1118 Louis VI. styles
himself "Ludovicus . . . . Francorum imperator augustus" (Luchaire, *Inst.
Mon.*, II., appendix 18, pp. 340-1, publishes the text in full.) M. Leroux in
the *Revue Historique*, XLIX. (1892), p. 255, *La Royauté française et le Saint
Empire Romain*, thinks that this innovation on the part of Louis le Gros was
after 1125, that is, after the death of Henry V. There is reason to think
that France, in theory at least, during the Middle Ages, was considered a part
of the Holy Roman Empire. When Odo II., Count of Blois and Champagne,
was defeated by the first Salic emperor, the Capetian king had no·ground upon
which he could deny the right of the emperor to carry his victory over upon
the soil of France. (Ranke, *Franzosische Geschichte*, Werke, VIII., p. 21.)
Philippe le Hardi was an unsuccessful aspirant for the imperial crown (Langlois,
Le Règne de Philippe le Hardi, pp. 64-70.) M. Leroux, in the article cited,
instances the French policy in Italy in the fourteenth century as showing the
intention of French kings to attain the imperial dignity. Even as late as the
sixteenth century (1519), the same hope lingered in the breast of Francis I.

[4] It did not become an exclusive ascription of the French crown until the
time of Louis. XI. *Cf.* Notice des MS., *Acad. des Belles-Lettres*, XXIX., p. 18.

But no prestige of title could avail against the sterner reality of a foe upon the north of France. The disastrous results of his intrigues in Normandy taught Louis VI. that the security of France lay in a territorial counterpoise to the barrier duchy. The influence of Suger had brought the grand fief of Blois-Champagne into the orbit of the king's influence in 1135.[1] Louis' position in the south was strong in the last years of his reign. The sire de Bourbon was his ally; the counts of Nevers and Auvergne were friendly, and Burgundy also was favorably disposed. Across the Loire lay the great duchy of Aquitaine with its numerous dependencies. Louis le Gros was the guardian of the young duchess Eleanor.[2] Destiny pointed to the union of France of the north and France of the south, in the marriage (24 July–1 August, 1137) of Eleanor and Louis the Young, the heir to the crown. The annexation of Aquitaine[3] was the consummation of the reign of Louis VI.[4] It doubled the

[1] Suger, 151, note 3. Ord. Vit., V., 48. For the importance of this event, see Luchaire, *Revue Historique*, XLVII. (1888), p. 274, *Louis le Gros et son Palatins · Annales*, No. 559, and Introd. xcii.

[2] On the will of William of Aquitaine, see *Acad. des Inscript.*, t. XLIII., p. 421. Consult also, Luchaire, *Manuel*, 217, d., and note 2.

[3] For the extent of Aquitaine, see Luchaire, *Inst. Mon.*, II., 261–2; Lalanne, *Dict. hist. de la France*, in loc., says : Le duché d'Aquitaine dont Eléanore était héritière, comprenait donc les comtés de Poitiers et du Limousin avec la suzeraineté de l'ancienne province ecclésiastique qui avait été l'Aquitaine secunde ; il s'étendait d'un côté sur la province d'Auch, le duché de Gascogne, les comtés de Bourdeaux et d'Agen, et de l'autre sur la partie de la Touraine située sur la rive gauche de la Loire. Il était suzerain de l'Auvergne, dans la province ecclésiastique de Bourges, autrefois l'Aquitaine secunde ; mais les autres pays dépendant de cette province relevaient des comtes de Toulouse, qui possédaient le Quercy, l'Albigeois, le Rouerque, le Gevaudan, le Velay—aussi quelques auteurs, pour distinguer ces deux parties de l'ancienne Aquitaine, ont donné le nom de Guyenne à celle dont les comtés des Poitiers étaient ducs. *Cf.* Vuitry I., 188. Hirsch, 15, is in error regarding Berry and Touraine. On the general subject, see Luchaire, *Annales*, Introd., cxi.–cxiv. The sources are numerous : Suger, 123 ff.; Ord. Vit., V., 81 ff.; H. F., XII., 68; 83–4; 116; 119; 125; 219; 409; 435, etc.

[4] At the next Christmas feast the king of what was really a new monarchy received his crown at Bourges . . . . Thus for one moment, as long as Louis and Eleanor remained man and wife, the lands south of the Loire became what they had never been before ; what, save for one moment of treachery (*i. e.*, the

size of the realm and carried with it a direct control over Guyenne, Saintonge and part of Poitou, with the suzerainty of Toulouse and its affiliated group, Auvergne, lower Touraine and Berry. And yet the acquisition, grand as it was, was less advantageous than Louis VI. thought. He thought he saw the shadow of an Anglican domination lifted since the young Louis was now king, or suzerain, of all the lands from Paris to the Pyrenees. But Touraine and Toulouse, Berry, La Marche and a portion of Poitou were not integral parts of the realm; they were more an embarrassment than an advantage.[1] The puissance of the monarchy lay north of the Loire,[2] where Louis VI. had ruled with firm hand for nearly thirty years.[3] Here was the core of the monarchy, the kernel of greater France, sound and solid. Louis le Gros died ere he saw the complete fulfilment of his plans.[4] Eleanor of Aquitaine was a queen before she set foot in Paris.[5] But when the ready brain and steady will were no more, neither the misrule of Louis VII. nor the fierce aggression of Henry Plantagenet

fraudulent dealings of Philip the Fair and Edward I.), they were never to be again for three hundred years—part of the domain of the king of Paris.—Freeman, *Norman Conquest*, V., 276-7.

[1] Luchaire, *Inst. Mon.*, II., 262. Consult also p. 22, note 1. For the revolt of Poitiers, see *Hist. du Roi Louis VII.*, c. vi.; *Inst. Mon.*, II., 171-2; Giry, *Établissements de Rouen*, I., 345-6.

[2] Pour la première fois, depuis la fondation de la dynastie, on avait vu se former et se grouper autour du prince un personnel de serviteurs intelligents, actifs et dévoués aux institutions monarchiques. Louis le Gros léguait à son fils, en même temps que Suger et Raoul de.Vermandois, des clercs expérimentés, déjà au courant des affaires de justice et de finances, et des chevaliers toujours prêts à se ranger sous la bannière du maître. Les grands offices étaient entre les mains de familles paisibles, dont la fidélité et l'obéissance ne faisaient plus doute. La curie, débarassée des éléments féodaux qui la troublaient, offrait enfin à la royauté l'instrument de pouvoir qui lui avait fait défaut jusqu'ici. On peut dire que le gouvernement capétien était fondé.—*Revue Hist.*, XXXVII. (1888), Luchaire, *Louis le Gros et son Palatins*, p. 277.

[3] "Dominium suum augens, pacem circumque superbos debellando reformans, xxx annis regnum Francia viriliter rexit."—*Continuator of Aimon*, H. F., XII., 123.

[4] Louis VI., died August 1, 1137. Suger, 129-30.

[5] Louis VII. entered Paris at the end of August 1137. *Hist. du Roi Louis VII.*, 147, note 4.

could undo the realm which almost he had created of his brain and fashioned of his hand.

When Louis VI. became king in 1108, he was already a man of maturity and administrative experience. The domestic policy of his reign is of more importance than his foreign relations. A policy of concentration was imperative for France at that time, owing to external circumstances. In the twelfth century feudalism reached the acme of its intensity. The principle of division thereby prevailing estranged the crown from the members of the great feudal constellation around it. This state of affairs was really an advantage to the monarchy, for it afforded it opportunity to strengthen itself at home, to develop itself intensively so that it could bear the shock of armed resistance when prepared to enter upon a wider field of achievement. To this work, which was destructive as well as constructive—for the power of the local baronage had first to be broken—Louis VI. brought the brain to plan, the will to dare and the energy to achieve. His position was one of difficulty. He was the heir of the accumulated sins, more of omission than of commission, of weaker rulers like Robert the Pious, Henry I. and Philip I.

The realm was small; the royal power dissipated; the crown tarnished. Like the greatness of Alfred of England, the greatness of Louis VI. must be measured by what he accomplished, of what he had to do. Louis devoted his life to the establishment of the crown in the regions of the Ile de France l'Orléannais, the Vexin and Picardy. His persevering and energetic conflicts, his little campaigns which were really hardly more than police expeditions, had thus an importance upon the future power of France far out of proportion to their appearance.

Louis' appreciation of law, his readiness to modify existing forms or to convert feudal institutions into instruments of crown power, are evidence of his creative ability. Even when those ideas ran counter to the vaster purpose of the papacy, France and the French monarchy were his first devotion. His reign fell in a time likely to be jeoparded by the papacy. The Concordat of Worms left Rome free to turn her eyes to France, but the con-

duct of Louis in its dignity, firmness and promptness saved the French monarchy from humiliation. And so by the adaptation of means to feasible ends, by the conscientious performance of the duty that lay nearest, Louis VI. from day to day gradually raised the crown from its ignominy, rid the kingdom of internal distresses, and strengthened the rods of royal authority, thereby leaving to his successors a solid center of repose, a sound core preserving those seeds of royal power and authority destined to blossom and bear fruit under the fostering watchfulness of Philip Augustus, St. Louis and Philip the Fair.

The End.

BIOGRAPHICAL NOTE.

JAMES WESTFALL THOMPSON was born at Pella, Iowa, U. S. A., 3 June, 1869 ; the second son of the late Rev. Abraham Thompson, a clergyman of the Reformed (Dutch) Church, and of Anna (Westfall) Thompson. His early education was received in the public schools of New York, and in the Rutgers Preparatory School, New Brunswick, N. J. He was graduated, with the degree of Bachelor of Arts, from Rutgers College, 22 June, 1892. He was matriculated in the Graduate School of the University of Chicago on 24 September, 1892, and was fellow in history, in that institution, 1893-5.